Inclusion

Related titles of interest

Closing the Inclusion Gap
Rita Cheminais
1 84312 085 2

Meeting Special Needs in . . . Series

The SENCO Handbook (4th edition)
Liz Cowne
1 84312 031 3

Inclusion at the Crossroads
Michael Farrell
1 84312 118 2

Support Services and Mainstream Schools
Mike Blamires and John Moore
1 84312 063 1

Inclusion

Meeting SEN in Secondary Classrooms

Sue Briggs

David Fulton Publishers

David Fulton Publishers Ltd
The Chiswick Centre, 414 Chiswick High Road, London W4 5TF

www.fultonpublishers.co.uk

First published in Great Britain in 2004 by David Fulton Publishers

10 9 8 7 6 5 4 3 2 1

David Fulton Publishers is a division of Granada Learning Limited, part of ITV plc.

Note: The right of Sue Briggs to be identified as the author of this work has been asserted by her in accordance with the Copyright, Designs and Patents Act 1988.

Copyright © Sue Briggs 2004

British Library Cataloguing in Publication Data
A catalogue record for this book is available from the British Library.

ISBN 1 84312 187 5

Typeset by Kenneth Burnley, Wirral, Cheshire
Printed and bound in Great Britain

Contents

Contents of CD

Chapter 2
First impressions checklist
'Go' symbol card
Writing with symbols
Secondary transition form

Chapter 3
Buddy sheet
Grouping checklist

Chapter 4
Pupil response recording form
Activity checklist
Observation form
Lesson differentiation form

Chapter 5
Training activities
Support record
Maths memory mat
Suggested contents of support toolbox

Chapter 7
ABC behaviour observation form
Behaviour prompt cards

Chapter 8
Accredited entry level courses and programmes
KS4 Curriculum Plan

Chapter 9
Secondary transfer questionnaire
Self-assessment record
Pupil comments
Self-reflection format
Symbol questionnaire
'Smiley' and 'sad' faces
Traffic lights template
Cue cards
Example of 'Me' bubbles

Acknowledgements

Warm thanks to all those who through their constant support have informed this book with their experience and wisdom. Special thanks to:

my critical friends: Hannah Briggs and Bridget Jones for their help and expertise;

Fran Jones for her friendship and professional encouragement;

Giulia Lampugnani and the teachers of the Circolo G. Falcone in Pisa who challenged my assumptions and proved that inclusion works;

Linda Evans of David Fulton Publishers for her patient guidance;

my daughters, for their love and encouraging telephone calls;

my husband, who has always supported this project with commitment and energy (and blessed English skills), and who has kept me supplied with endless cups of coffee.

The author and publisher acknowledge the following organizations for the use of illustrations within the book:

Widgit Software Ltd, Cambridge, for the use of symbols;

Gill and Mike Kennard for the Signalong illustrations;

Crick Software Ltd (www.cricksoft.com) for the grid on p. 50 (reproduced by permission).

*This book is dedicated to my fifteen-year-old ginger tom, Catty,
who every day lies dozing in the window by my computer.*

Foreword

Mainstream schools are now admitting pupils with a diverse range of abilities and individual needs. This book has been written for subject teachers, SENCOs and teaching assistants in mainstream secondary schools to support the inclusion of pupils with significant, complex or severe learning difficulties. Advisory teachers and inspectors also will find the information valuable for their work in supporting schools.

Inclusion looks different in every school. You need to find strategies that work in your classroom for *your* pupils. If something doesn't work with one group, try it with another. Inclusion isn't a fixed state; it's a process. It may help to think of it as a journey: it may take a long time to reach the destination, and some people will travel faster than others, but as we become more confident and begin to enjoy the challenge we find out what works for us and ditch things that do not. The key is to celebrate and enjoy the triumphs and learn from things that turn out to be less successful. It is always possible to learn from other people's experience. The ideas and suggestions that follow come from many years of working with pupils with severe learning difficulties in special and mainstream schools.

Note

The accompanying CD contains downloadable versions of all record sheets, cue cards and other useful resources which can be amended to meet individual needs. For a full list see p. vi.

Introduction

Inclusion and recent legislative changes

From September 2002 new legislation brought a subtle but important change for those of us involved in the inclusion of pupils with learning difficulties. The Special Educational Needs and Disability Act (2001) amended Part 4 the Disability Discrimination Act (1995) to include schools and educational services. This Act strengthens the right of parents of children with learning difficulties and other disabilities and special educational needs to choose a mainstream school placement for their child, so long as that is compatible with the efficient education of other children. The new duties make it unlawful for responsible bodies to discriminate without justification against disabled pupils, and prospective pupils, in all aspects of school life. The principle behind the legislation is that, wherever possible, disabled people should have the same opportunities as non-disabled people in their access to education. The duties cover admissions, education and associated services, and exclusions. The 'responsible body' for a school is ultimately liable and responsible for the actions of all employees, and anyone working with the authority of the school. In maintained schools the responsible body is usually the governing body. The requirements of the Act are anticipatory; schools are required to plan for pupils with disabilities *even where there currently are no pupils with disabilities*.

Section 1 of the Act defines a person with a disability as:

someone who has a physical or mental impairment which has an effect on his or her ability to carry out normal day-to-day activities. The effect must be:
- Substantial (that is more than trivial); and
- Long-term (that is, has lasted or is likely to last for at least a year, or for the rest of the life of the person affected); and
- Adverse. (Disability Rights Commission 2002)

Physical or mental impairment includes sensory impairments and also hidden impairments (for example, mental illness or mental health problems, learning difficulties, dyslexia and conditions such as diabetes or epilepsy). People with severe disfigurements are also covered within the Act. The Disability Rights Commission has published an excellent Code of Practice for Schools which contains useful case studies that may be used to train school staff. The new duties require schools to draw up accessibility plans to improve over time access to the education in schools. The plans must address three elements of planned improvements in access for disabled pupils:

- improvements in access to the curriculum;
- physical improvements to increase access to education and associated services;
- improvements in the provision of information in a range of formats for disabled pupils.

This book supports schools in the first of these elements: making improvements in accessibility to the curriculum for pupils with significant, complex and severe learning difficulties. The term 'pupils with learning difficulties' is used throughout and is meant to include all pupils with significant, complex and severe learning difficulties.

The Index for Inclusion

The Index for Inclusion (see Booth *et al.* 2000) was distributed to all maintained schools by the Department for Education and Skills but has been an underused resource in many cases. It supports schools in the review of their policies, practices and procedures, and their development of an inclusive approach.

The Index involves all members of the school community as equal partners in the process; governors, senior management, parents, pupils, teachers, support staff, and the community. They are helped to identify areas for development, through meetings and questionnaires. After investigating all aspects of school life, the Index gives a framework for developing an action plan to make the school more inclusive. By bringing the community together in this way, the process ensures that all have a stake in making the action plan successful. Schools that have used the Index have found the process challenging and sometimes uncomfortable, but the result is always valuable. Where it has been used as part of the school improvement process – looking at inclusion in the widest sense – it has been a great success.

The National Curriculum Inclusion Statement

The National Curriculum Inclusion Statement is included in the primary handbook, and in each of the subject documents for secondary schools. It outlines how teachers can modify the National Curriculum Programmes of Study as necessary to provide all pupils with relevant and appropriately challenging work at each key stage.

The Inclusion Statement reaffirms that schools have a responsibility to provide a broad and balanced curriculum for all pupils, and that all pupils are entitled to the National Curriculum as the basis of the curriculum. Schools are also able to provide other curricular and therapeutic opportunities *outside* the National Curriculum to meet individual needs.

The Statement sets out three key principles of inclusion:

- Setting suitable learning challenges;
- Responding to pupils' diverse learning needs; and
- Overcoming potential barriers to learning for individuals and groups of pupils.

Setting suitable learning challenges

The National Curriculum Programmes of Study set out what pupils should be taught at each key stage, but teachers need to teach the knowledge, skills and understanding in ways that suit their own pupils' abilities (DfEE 1999). All pupils need to experience success and achieve their individual potential. Pupils with learning difficulties are no exception, even though their individual potential may be different from others of the same age. Expecting all pupils always to do the same work will ensure that some will find the work too easy, while for others the challenge will be about right. However, there will still be a significant group in any class for whom the challenge is inappropriate, and who will fail. If failure occurs regularly, students stop caring and begin to lack motivation, become disillusioned, and are likely to be disruptive. It is a teacher's responsibility to ensure that all pupils succeed, and a test of their skill to design lessons and activities that are appropriately differentiated.

Responding to pupils' diverse learning needs

Teachers will need to use a range of teaching strategies to match individual learning styles with a variety of activities within each lesson. It is possible to base work on objectives from earlier or later key stages to help pupils make progress. Particularly useful is the 'tracking back' method (Chapter 4) linking age-appropriate activities to individually appropriate objectives. This method gives teachers the flexibility to devise interesting and challenging lessons that match the need for a greater degree of differentiation for a more diverse group of students. The National Curriculum Programmes of Study that match pupils' chronological age can be used as *contexts* for learning, and as starting points for planning learning experiences appropriate to a pupil's age and requirements. It is important to have high expectations, especially of pupils with severe learning difficulties. Those expectations will drive target setting for subjects, and encourage pupils to greater achievement. All children bring to school their own individual strengths and interests which influence the way in which they learn (DfEE 1999). When planning for diversity, teachers need to be aware of the child's experiences and motivations. Planning approaches that allow pupils fully and effectively to take part in lessons will raise attainment for all the class and minimise disruptive behaviour.

Teachers need to respond to pupils' diverse learning needs by:

- creating effective learning environments that secure motivation and concentration;
- planning appropriate activities;
- using a range of teaching strategies;
- managing support for pupils, both in terms of staff and resources;
- using appropriate assessment approaches;
- setting suitable targets for learning.

Overcoming barriers to learning and assessment

There are many events and conditions in pupils' lives that create barriers to their learning; hunger, emotional upset, illness, family separation, bereavement, etc. For pupils with learning difficulties or a disability, the barriers to learning are often very evident. Some pupils may be contending with additional barriers, such as hunger or family separation, which may be less evident. Schools need to be sure that inflexible systems and policies do not create yet more barriers. Curriculum planning and assessment must take into account the type and extent of pupils' difficulties. For most pupils the need for curriculum access will be met through greater differentiation of tasks and materials. Some pupils with learning difficulties will need access to more specialist equipment or approaches. These would include written materials in Braille for a pupil with a visual impairment, or the use of materials and resources that pupils can access through sight, touch, sound, smell or taste.

Teachers should take specific action to provide access to learning for pupils with learning difficulties by:

- providing help with communication, language and literacy;
- planning to develop understanding through all available senses and experiences;
- planning for full participation in learning and physical and practical activities;
- helping pupils manage their behaviour so they can take part in learning effectively and safely;
- at Key Stage 4, helping pupils to prepare for the world of work;
- helping pupils manage their emotions, especially trauma and stress (DfEE 1999)

The Inclusion Statement stresses that not all pupils with disabilities have special educational needs. Teachers should plan to enable pupils with disabilities to participate as fully and effectively as possible. Potential areas of difficulty should, as far as possible, be identified and addressed at the outset of work without recourse to the formal provisions for disapplication from all or part of the National Curriculum.

Entitlement

Entitlement to the National Curriculum is very important for pupils with severe learning difficulties. Until 1944 these children were deemed to be ineducable, and came under the responsibility of the Health Service. Large numbers of children and adults with learning difficulties or disabilities were placed in long stay hospitals and asylums. Children were separated from their families and local communities for months and years at a time. It was only in 1944 that local education authorities were required to find out which children in their area had special educational needs, and to make appropriate provision for them. From 1944 to 1970 children with severe learning difficulties were placed in training centres rather than schools, and had no access to qualified teachers. The Education (Handicapped Children) Act of 1970 meant that for the first time, all children with disabilities were brought within the framework of special education with the right to be taught by trained teachers.

Those working in special education argued long and hard that special schools should be required to use the National Curriculum as the basis of the curriculum. It was feared that children with severe learning difficulties could easily be forgotten or marginalised, and that exclusion from the National Curriculum would be tantamount to exclusion from the education service. (Mittler in Fagg *et al.* 1990).

Inclusion as part of school improvement

Inclusion all too often is seen as an issue about special educational needs, or race, or gender. But inclusion is much more about making schools more humane and pleasant places in which to work and learn – for everyone. It is about improving schools from both the academic and the social point of view and there is a growing body of evidence to show that making schools more inclusive, more responsive to diverse needs, actually drives up examination results.

Box 1.1	Clearing the ramp

One morning in January children arrive at school after a night of heavy snow. The caretaker is busy clearing snow away from the steps that lead to the temporary class-room. Peter, who uses a wheelchair, is very cold and asks the caretaker if he would clear the ramp so he can go into class. The caretaker tells him to wait because he must clear the steps for the others first, then he will clear the ramp.

Peter's friend, Kuli, then suggests, 'But if you clear the ramp, we can all go in.'

Inclusion 'clears the ramp' for everyone (Giangreco 2000).

Parents as partners

There are as many types of parents and families as there are children in our schools. This book uses the word 'parents' to include all those adults who have the important role of caring for children. Parents range from those who are extremely committed to the school and their children's education, those who are interested but very busy, and who rely on the school to keep them informed, to those parents who because of circumstances or their own past experiences, either feel uncomfortable in the school environment or do not value education for their children.

An inclusive school is one where all parents are drawn into the life of the school and see themselves as a vital element of their child's education. The sense of isolation that sometimes develops in pupils with learning difficulties is often mirrored in their parents. Some parents become very defensive about school, often with good reason. Breaking down those defences will be difficult and time consuming, but it is essential that a close working relationship is established between the school and the parents/carers if the long term placement is to be successful. Communication with families will need to be frequent and regular, and based on goodwill. Anything that takes up too much time will remain undone, with both sides feeling let down. Here are some suggestions for developing positive communication between home and school that is effective, as well as being time efficient.

Home–school diary

A daily home–school diary is a good way of keeping in touch with parents but it is time consuming and in secondary schools difficult to manage. A code system that is written into the homework diary after each lesson is one way round this. A letter or a number next to each subject gives parents simple information that may be followed up at consultation evenings or on the telephone. The following are examples.

Academic work
- A = Tried hard and met the lesson targets.
- B = Understood most of the key information and met some of the lesson targets.
- C = Found the work very difficult. Did not meet the lesson targets. Follow up at home.

Behaviour
- 1 = Good behaviour, stayed on task all lesson.
- 2 = Needed support to stay on task.
- 3 = Some disruptive behaviour. Please contact school.

For example, Michaela might have A2 for English, B1 in history and C2 for maths. Her parents would know where she had difficulties and could support her with the maths homework to make sure she understood the concepts in time for the next lesson.

With this system parents can receive concise information about how their child is working in school. The majority have no behaviour problems and the letter code would be enough for those pupils. The teacher or teaching assistant could write additional comments or add stickers or stars as appropriate.

Personal organisers and diaries
Personal organisers or diaries are a more age-appropriate method of communicating with parents, particularly for older students. A sticky note attached to the page for the day will give the necessary information simply and discreetly.

Dictaphones
Dictaphones are now relatively cheap and using them is an easy and time efficient way of passing messages between home and school. Pupils love to use them and for some children they can be a key factor in developing speech.

Email

Information can be passed to several sets of parents at once using email. Copies of schemes of work or lesson plans can be sent out to enable parents to reinforce concepts and support homework. Email is more informal than other written methods and may be less threatening to some parents. Replying on email is also quick and easy and will encourage busy parents to respond.

Telephone calls

Some parents need an even more personal approach. When a pupil has worked well, tried hard, or achieved a personal goal, a telephone call to the parents will be really appreciated by families. Building up direct positive contacts is a way of developing trust between school and parents, and will make future problems easier to resolve. A phone call often sorts out minor misunderstandings and is especially helpful to parents who themselves have problems with reading and numeracy. A couple of timely calls may avoid a great deal of paperwork and acrimony.

Home visits

Home visits are rarely a feature of secondary school practice, but they are the most effective way of developing positive communication with the parents of pupils with learning difficulties. The visits should start in the year before the pupil transfers to the secondary school, and will need to continue for at least the first year of the placement. Parents will give teachers and teaching assistants the background to the child's learning and behaviour. This understanding will inform target setting, and will make Individual Education Plans more specific to the child's needs.

Meeting the pupil in the home context can have other benefits. Pupils are much more likely to behave well in class when they know their teachers and parents are talking together and working together.

Not why, but how

Recent legislation – and a forest of books – has addressed the 'why' question about inclusion. This book sets out to give schools some help with the 'how'.

Chapter 2 looks at how mainstream secondary schools can prepare to welcome and include pupils with learning difficulties.

2 Welcoming pupils with learning difficulties

We all need to feel wanted, whether that is being made to feel welcome when we move to a new area, attend a church for the first time, join a club, or just when buying a paper from the newsagents. How we are made to feel welcome can be difficult to pinpoint, but it is that initial positive contact that makes us want to return. As teachers we get only one chance to make that first impression and extend a warm welcome to pupils.

When a group of pupils were asked what made them feel welcome, their answers were refreshing and simple:

- 'A smile'.
- 'A handshake'.
- 'They treat me as if they like me'.
- 'Someone to show me where to go'.
- 'When someone spends time with me'.

These responses give clues about what makes people feel welcome when they visit schools, and how that welcome can be achieved.

All schools aim to be open and welcoming and most spend time and resources to create a positive first impression. Within such a busy environment it can be difficult to maintain a consistent level of welcome. Parents arriving by appointment at 10 a.m., when everyone is in class, are likely to get the full works – smiles from the administration staff, a warm greeting, the offer of coffee, comfortable chairs on which to wait, information about the school to read, and a prompt response from the member of staff concerned. However, if parents were to arrive at 2.30 p.m., during a lesson change on the day of the school play, would the welcome be the same?

The first welcome into the secondary school is so important for children with learning difficulties and their parents or carers. By the time children reach this transition stage they will probably have experienced rejection and discrimination on many occasions. Some parents feel they have to battle every step of the way for their child, seeing schools and local education authorities as obstacles in their fight for a mainstream education. To be made to feel welcome as they walk through the door gives such a good basis to starting a new school career.

When speaking about transfer to secondary school, the parents' greatest fear is that their child will not be able to cope. When we unpick what parents mean by 'being able to cope', they rarely mean coping with lessons. Parents fear their child will not be able to cope with the apparently chaotic environment that they often see on a first visit to the school. A most effective way to test the first impressions given by your school is to ask governors and teachers from other schools to visit unannounced at different times within a week. If the purpose of this exercise is to get it right for prospective parents – do it before they come. The experiences can be fed back to the whole staff and any areas for development may then be addressed. The 'First Impressions Checklist' on the accompanying CD can be used as a starting point for assessing visits.

The ethos of the school

In schools successfully including pupils with severe learning difficulties, the foundation of that success is the commitment of the head teacher and other senior staff to the broad principle of inclusion. The emphasis on inclusion is an impetus to raising standards for all pupils in the school (Ofsted 2003). This impetus is combined with a wholehearted determination from all staff to work for the greatest possible success for all, and a willingness to meet individual specific needs.

As part of all inspections Ofsted now looks at how a school's ethos promotes tolerance and respect for difference and diversity. Successful schools do this by celebrating and valuing the success of all pupils, fostering mutual respect, and raising self-esteem. The words 'inclusive ethos' in the school mission statement is a start, but that ethos has to be rolled out into the practice of everyone in the school – staff and pupils.

We bring all kinds of past experiences, beliefs and values with us to work, and that is just the same for people working in schools. For some, the concept of children with learning difficulties being taught in mainstream schools is challenging. Teachers and teaching assistants are already very busy people. They don't understand why they should have the extra work of including a child with learning difficulties in their lessons, when there is a 'perfectly good' special school down the road. Feelings of inadequacy in meeting these children's needs come to the fore – and often also a fear of the unknown. Teachers tell of their concerns about keeping discipline; about not being able to communicate; about pupils' personal care and toileting; about medication; about epilepsy; . . . about a pupil who is so 'different'. These worries are natural and understandable but they are not reasons for exclusion. All concerns can be addressed and many problems resolved before a pupil arrives, by talking to parents and support services and by putting suitable training in place.

There have always been children with special needs in mainstream schools. The difference now is that many of the children have a wider range of special needs, and in some cases they may even look a little different. A pupil with Down's Syndrome can be more able than a child without such an obvious learning difficulty, yet a placement in a mainstream school may be questioned before the child's true ability is understood. A child with cerebral palsy may be very able, with their only barrier to learning being a different mode of communication.

Looking through the learning difficulty to see the child within is the real key to including pupils with special needs. These children have a great deal to offer our schools if we can learn how to recognise and celebrate their gifts. *First and foremost, these are children, and we are educators – with a mission to teach and nurture.*

Language and terminology

The area of special educational need and disability is a minefield of ever-changing acronyms and jargon . . .

'The SENCO and the EP from the LSS wrote an IEP for a pupil with ADHD.'

These terms are a form of shorthand that can be useful among professionals, but used without care they can be intensely intimidating to parents (and some teachers), and do not make clear either the pupil's needs or the school's intentions. They may serve to exclude and alienate parents and carers, and sometimes even alienate professionals from other agencies.

The words we use when we talk about pupils with learning difficulties or a disability *do* have an impact on the pupils themselves and how they are perceived and treated. There is a useful rule of thumb when trying to decide what to say or write, and that is to make sure the pupil is not defined by their disability or special need. Put the pupil first in the sentence, and the disability or special need afterwards. For example, say, 'a pupil with Down's Syndrome', rather than 'a Down's Syndrome pupil'.

Some words have negative connotations and are no longer in general use – words such as 'handicapped', having a basis in disabled people going 'cap in hand' for charity. Medical terms, such as 'spastic', 'cretin', or 'cripple', were once commonly used to describe people with special needs or a disability, but are now seen as inappropriate, particularly as they are often used as terms of abuse.

In general, the term 'a person with learning difficulties' or 'a person with special needs' is used, and this form of wording covers most eventualities. It is easy to become so interested in a pupil's particular syndrome that we miss seeing the real person. A teacher once said in a meeting that his pupil was 'more David than Down's'; the child's personality, individual experiences and support network being of far greater importance than the medical diagnosis. However, no one is perfect. Everyone is prone to a slip of the tongue, and it would be terrible if fear of using the wrong terminology discouraged adults from talking to, or being involved with, young people with special educational needs or disability.

Training for staff and pupils

It is many years now since there has been specialist initial teacher training in special educational needs. All trainee teachers have some training for special needs, but this is often as little as a few hours of lectures as part of a one year PGCE course. This level of knowledge does not adequately prepare teachers to work with the full range of pupils with special needs usually found in mainstream schools, let alone those with severe and complex learning difficulties. It falls to local education authorities, and schools themselves, to arrange training for all staff.

Careful preparation for admission should be started well before the pupil is to arrive, if successful inclusion is to be achieved. Teachers and teaching assistants need to have training on the particular needs of the pupils with severe learning difficulties who are to join the school community, and given guidance on appropriate teaching methods, learning activities, and specialist or adapted materials.

Training ought to be offered at a variety of levels. This should include:

- Disability awareness training – This training will help staff to understand the issues relating to disability and diversity in society. It will support them in developing other pupils' acceptance and understanding of diversity within the school. The Commission for Equality and Human Rights recommends suitable trainers, and the cost may be shared if several schools train staff together.
- General information for all staff, including non-teaching staff members – This will include an overview of the pupil's particular strengths and needs, the behaviour strategies used in the child's current school, and any relevant health and safety issues.
- Advice and guidance for subject teachers and teaching assistants on how to differentiate and adapt lessons and resources.
- Specialist training to address a pupil's specific needs – To teach staff how to sign, use symbols or a communication aid, and/or administer medication.
- On-going opportunities – For meeting colleagues and the SENCO, advisory teacher, or educational psychologist, to discuss successful strategies and plan for the future.

Liaison with primary schools

Liaison with feeder primary schools is an important aspect of the secondary school's responsibilities, both in terms of general forward planning, and where there are potential pupils with special needs. Regular meetings give the secondary school knowledge of potential pupils several years in advance. This means that many issues of access can be addressed in good time, and should not pose problems in the year before – and certainly not the year after – a pupil arrives. A member of staff must be assigned to lead the liaison with the primary school. This is often a part of the role of the SENCO, but a Year 7 tutor would also be suitable, especially if he or she will eventually be the form tutor for the pupil with learning difficulties.

Transition reviews of a pupil's Statement of Special Educational Needs take place two academic years before transfer, that is Year 5 in primary schools and Year 7 in middle schools. These reviews are of key importance. Decisions made at transition reviews will shape a pupil's secondary education and will determine many future life opportunities.

Preparatory visits

Parental visits

It is advisable for parents/carers of children with severe learning difficulties to visit numerous schools in the months leading up to the transition review. If they have visited all potential schools they will be able to make an informed choice based on their knowledge of the child and what they, the parents/carers, want from the school.

Implied negatives

When parents of children with special needs visit a prospective school for their child, they will be very sensitive to the responses of the head teacher and other staff members. It does not need to be the blunt, 'Oh, I don't think we could meet those needs in this school'. Parents all too often report that head teachers or SENCOs recommend that they visit a particular special school or a school with a resourced provision or 'unit', implying that a different school would be a better placement for the pupil.

The negative is often more subtle however:

'We have a very high proportion of more able pupils in our school'
'We expect all our pupils to pass five or more GCSEs'
'Do you think your daughter could cope in this school?'

These may be valid points about the school, but saying such things may make the parent/carer of a child with special needs feel their child is unwelcome.

Schools should give parents information about the school's pastoral system, the special needs provision – or even the merits of the drama department. Identifying these aspects will help parents leave the school with positive feelings and provide the basis for making an informed decision.

Pupil visits

Getting to know a secondary school well before transfer is very important if a pupil is to have a successful placement. This is most easily achieved by arranging additional preparatory visits in the academic year before transfer. Obviously these visits can only take place where a secondary placement has been agreed well in advance. The importance of thinking well ahead cannot be overemphasised. Parents need to have chosen a school before the transition review in order to give time for preparatory visits to be arranged.

Where secondary schools have regular contact with their feeder primaries the process will be much simpler. Pupils will be used to visiting the 'big school' as part of usual practice. But even where primary and secondary schools share a campus, that contact can be superficial.

It may take some children up to two years to settle fully into a new school. This is particularly the case where they transfer from a small primary school to a large secondary. Even pupils without learning difficulties often find it hard to fit into the new community with its written – and unwritten – rules and new social norms. Merely moving from one class to another, through busy corridors, carrying all the equipment they need for that day, is daunting for many children.

The first visit

The visits need to start early in the autumn term, with a joint visit for pupil and parents/carers after pupils have left at the end of the school day. Coming to terms with the size and layout of the buildings before having to deal with the social demands of the school is very helpful. Schools can suggest to parents/carers that they bring a camera with them on the visit, and take photographs of different areas of the school. This gives the child opportunities to look at the photographs and ask questions at home. The family can make a scrapbook about the school to which the child can add after each visit. A key worker or mentor should be assigned to the pupil on this first visit. The key worker will be the parent/carer's first point of contact, and will be responsible for the transition and, where possible, the pupil's continuing placement.

The second joint visit

This should follow on quite soon and should take place during the school day. The visit should be unhurried, with plenty of opportunities for all to ask questions. The child should not be expected to take part in any activities at this stage. A prospective pupil will best be left to watch and absorb the atmosphere in the security of their parents' company. Any access issues may be discussed at this visit, giving the school plenty of time to make any necessary reasonable adjustments.

Open day

The family could visit again for the school open day or evening. This will give them the opportunity to meet other parents and the child to meet potential future classmates.

Class visits

An invitation to the child's class to visit the secondary school for an art day, or a Christmas concert, will create positive associations without singling out the pupil with special needs. Concert programmes or completed art work could be added to the scrapbook started after the first visit.

Small group visits

In the spring term the links with the pupil's class can be developed further and small group visits for specific lessons arranged. The pupil with special needs, along with two friends and a teaching assistant, could join Year 7 classes for music or drama, depending on individual particular interests. Worksheets or play scripts could again be added to the scrapbook, building up the information on the school, and increasing confidence.

Joining Year 7 lessons

In the summer term regular weekly visits will need to take place. These visits should include time spent with classes in the library, science laboratories, design and technology workshop, and the gym. Some of these visits should be for the pupil and a teaching assistant, some for small groups, and some for the whole year group. Information about safety in these areas can be included in the scrapbook so that the pupil is prepared for the start of the new school year.

The form room

Before the end of the summer term the pupil should be shown the new form room and given a place to keep personal belongings – a drawer or a box in a cupboard containing a favourite book, a soft toy from home, drawing paper and pens; that is, anything that will be familiar and recognisable when the pupil starts at the school after the summer holiday.

A video of the school

A short video of a school day will give the pupil something to watch during the summer holiday and prepare for the transition. The video will start the pupil and his or her family talking about the new school, and will build awareness and realistic expectations of how that secondary school operates.

Time spent preparing for transition is never wasted, and the more comfortable and confident the child feels about the school the more successful will be their long term placement.

Additional information for pupils with learning difficulties

Pupils with learning difficulties will need specific information in preparation for the transition in addition to the usual information that schools send to new parents. The most effective way of giving this information is to create a transition pack jointly with the pupil and the primary school.

The pack will need to contain the usual information such as school prospectus, uniform details, etc. Possible additional information:

- a plan or map of the school campus
- a short video of the school in action
- a list of teachers and teaching assistants, with their photographs
- a symbolic or pictorial timetable
- a list of the school rules
- a homework diary.

What do teachers and teaching assistants need to know?

Transition forms

The transition form is a vital document to give schools access to detailed information about new pupils. For the transition of pupils with learning difficulties, the SENCO needs as much relevant information as possible in order to make decisions about groupings and support for individuals. Figure 2.1 is an example of a completed transition form. A photocopiable blank transition form is provided on the accompanying CD.

Information for subject teachers

The information given to subject teachers is crucial to a successful placement. Merely knowing that a pupil is at School Action Plus is insufficient. Teachers require information about a child's particular strengths and needs. However, too much information can be a burden at the start of a busy term and one side of A4 paper should be enough to give the important details. The form should include a photograph of the pupil, interests, dislikes, access issues, usual mode of communication, level of support needed, and any information particular to the subject area, for example, speed of changing before PE.

The first day in the new school

Where a child has visited the school on several occasions it is useful to ask them to help to show other new pupils around the school. This serves two purposes. Firstly, the pupil will be pleased to be given responsibility and will gain self-esteem. Secondly, other pupils will have a positive first impression of their classmate with learning difficulties.

Even if the pupil has a teaching assistant assigned to him or her, try not to make the support too overt, especially on that first day. The pupil needs to

BRADTHORPE HIGH SCHOOL

Y7 TRANSITION FORM	Name: Karen Smith	Date of birth: 23/6/93	Transferring from: St Luke's

Home address:
7 Blair Road
Bradthorpe

Tel: 01234 567 891
Email: g.reynolds@aol.com

Names of parents/carers and siblings:
Mum: Gillian Reynolds
Dad: Paul Smith
Sister: Gemma Reynolds
Brother: Shane Smith

Pets:
Dog: Sheba
Cat: Blackie
Fish: Nemo

Contacts at liaison school:

Mrs Phillips: (SENCO)

Miss Lewis: Class teacher

Likes and dislikes:
(Karen)
I like dancing and riding my trike.
Writing is hard. I can count to 100.

Tests results:
Teacher assessment:
Karen is working at P8 for reading and writing and Level 1A for speaking and listening and numeracy.

Last book read: A Day in London
Oxford Reading Tree Stage 8 – Magpies

Talents and interests:
Karen is good at singing and loves all music activities. She goes to Riding for the Disabled classes on Saturdays. She can steer her horse and trot.

Special needs/disability:
Karen has cerebral palsy and severe learning difficulties.

Code of Practice: School Action
School Action +
Statement

Friends:
(Karen):
Narinder is my friend and Amy. I don't like Lee. I sit next to Narinder.
Mode of communication:
Speech and electronic communication aid.

Access:
Wheelchair
Kay walker
Laptop
Medication:
Tegretol (carbamazepine) – at home
Rectal diazepam (0.5mg) – kept in school

FIGURE 2.1   Example of a completed Year 7 transition form

become used to being independent in the classroom and around the school and it is best to start as you mean to go on. This is also important in determining how the pupil is perceived by others. All the class will be unsure in the new setting, and if they are encouraged to help each other, they will naturally give support to the pupil with learning difficulties. A planned buddy scheme will ensure this mutual support happens and may be the start of future social groupings.

Pastoral support

Where a key worker or mentor has been assigned to the family in the year before transfer, that person will already be a familiar face by the time the child starts at the new school. Where a pupil has individual support, the mentor should be someone other than the child's own teaching assistant. A regular meeting with the pupil once a week should be enough to address any difficulties or misunderstandings that may arise.

Safe haven

Many secondary schools set aside a room or area of the school where pupils are allowed to go at breaks and lunchtimes if they find it difficult to be part of the 'rough and tumble' outside. Some pupils use these areas occasionally when they need to finish off work, or if it is too cold for them outside. Others will need a 'sanctuary' for much of the unstructured time in school. While most lessons are well ordered and are focused on the teacher, breaks are intensely social times where pupils are expected to interact with others, play games or just gossip. For pupils with an incomplete understanding of spoken English, or who do not understand irony, sarcasm or jokes, the usual banter between students can be misconstrued as bullying. Pupils with learning difficulties, and especially those with autistic spectrum disorders, need to learn how to interact with others in conversation or games before being expected to join in.

The safe haven is a useful place for pupils to begin to learn these skills before being encouraged to venture out onto the playground. The time in the safe haven can also be used to prepare for forthcoming lessons, read social stories (see Chapter 7), or practise important skills such as typing.

It is also worth extending the concept of a safe haven into class time. Pupils with behavioural, emotional and social difficulties, and those with autistic spectrum disorders, often have times when their level of anxiety is so high they cannot manage their own behaviour in class. Simply having a way of signalling this to the teacher, such as holding up a red card or a 'go' symbol (see Figure 2.2, also downloadable from CD) and then having somewhere safe to go, gives the pupil an escape route and means that fewer classes are disrupted.

The safe haven would need to be staffed at all times but it will be worthwhile if this results in fewer disrupted lessons. Further, this room should be kept separate from any punishment room, as challenging behaviour or negative connotations would devalue its purpose.

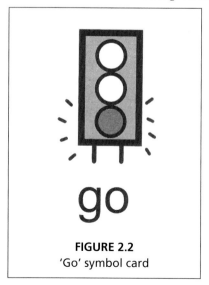

FIGURE 2.2
'Go' symbol card

Communicating with pupils who have learning difficulties

Only seven per cent of our understanding of language comes from the words we hear. The bulk of the meaning comes from the context, facial expression, eye gaze, gesture and body language. Communication is about much more than speech, and for students with communication difficulties it is essential to maximise other paths to understanding.

A useful starting point is to ask someone who knows the pupil well to help you communicate. Parents are best placed to give this help as they will have developed communication with their child over the years. When a pupil communicates by speech but has articulation difficulties, you will find that you gradually tune in to their way of speaking. However, when a pupil uses signing or a communication aid it can take longer to establish full communication and some training will need to be given to key adults working with the pupil.

Here are some helpful tips for communicating with a pupil with learning difficulties.

- When you want to tell the pupil something, or to ask them a question, say their name first. For example, 'Katy, take out your homework diary'. This gains the pupil's attention and lets them know that they need to listen.
- When you ask a question, give the pupil time to process the question and then to formulate the answer. A slow count of ten is usually about the right length of time.
- If you think a pupil has not understood, try not to rephrase the question too soon. It will be interpreted as a separate question and will cause confusion.
- Use simple straightforward language in short sentences. This doesn't mean talking down to pupils but will help them understand what you want.
- Most pupils with learning difficulties are visually much stronger than they are aurally. Use objects, photographs, pictures or symbols to support speech and these will get the message across much more easily.
- When first meeting a pupil use minimum eye contact. Some pupils find eye contact threatening, especially those pupils with an autistic spectrum disorder.
- If a pupil is trying to tell you something and you don't understand, ask them to repeat what they have said. If you still don't understand, say so, but ask them to tell someone they know better who might be more 'tuned in'. Look around for clues, ask the pupil to point to or draw something that might help.
- Try not to finish off pupils' sentences, even if you are sure you know what they are going to say. It is annoying, and you could be wrong. By all means smile and encourage them to keep trying, but if they think they don't have to communicate – they won't bother next time!
- Give validity and respect to pupils' opinions.

Modes of communication

There are many different modes of communication that people use, either on their own or in combinations.

Vocalisation

Where pupils have limited or no speech, they may use other vocal sounds to attempt to communicate, as in the case study below about James, who desperately wanted to make himself understood and used the sound 'h' for hat in conjunction with gesture.

Facial expression

Facial expression is probably the most effective form of communication after speech, but it requires a relatively high level of sophistication to understand all possible nuances. The movements that are used to change meaning are very subtle, and pupils with learning difficulties often use a limited range of expressions. It is also worth remembering that facial expression does not always reflect what a person with learning difficulties is thinking. Pupils with autistic spectrum disorders will have difficulties both in understanding facial expression, and in using it effectively as part of communication.

FIGURE 2.3   Facial expression drawings

Physical movement

When all else fails, pupils will often take an adult by the hand to show what they want. Pupils with autistic spectrum disorders often use this mode of communication.

Gesture

Some pupils who have little or no speech will compensate by using more gesture, but this can be very idiosyncratic and it will take some time to begin to know what the pupil means.

CASE STUDY | **James**

James has a severe communication disorder and communicates using gestures and some Signalong signs. On a hot day in the summer he approached a teaching assistant on duty in the playground. He was clearly distressed, tapping his head with the flat of his hand and making h..h..h.. sounds. The teaching assistant had had no signing training and so ignored him. One of James's classmates then came over and told the teaching assistant that James wanted his hat because he was very hot.

In this situation the signing was a red herring and caused the teaching assistant not to respond to James's attempt to communicate. James was distressed and simply wanted to let the adult know that he needed his hat. He used natural gesture and the initial sound that he knew.

Signing

The use of signing is an effective way of supporting communication for people with learning difficulties. It adds a visual component to speech and formalises the use of gesture. Students with learning difficulties are not expected to sign every word. They are taught signs that will support their communication at whatever level that may be. Some students will use only a few signs that are really important to them, while others use a large number of signs that support a developing understanding and complexity of language.

The two most commonly used signing systems are Signalong and Makaton. Both these systems are a form of sign-supported English, based on British Sign Language. They are used in addition to speech and follow the word order of spoken English. It is possible to link signing to the use of symbols to develop literacy.

Signing can be effective only where a sufficient number of people in the school, both staff and pupils, know some signs. Hiring a trainer for an in-service training session will give the staff basic understanding of the system and will teach them how to read the manuals. Some schools set up signing clubs at lunchtimes or after school. Such clubs teach many pupils this valuable skill that also supports the communication of pupils with learning difficulties.

Body language

Body language is a very powerful but sophisticated communication tool. Our posture as we stand or sit, or how near or far away we stand from a person, can change the meaning of what we say. In conversation we often mirror the stance of the person we are talking to, lean towards someone we like, or cross our arms when we feel defensive. Students with learning difficulties often do not understand other people's body language, and rely too much on the words used. They often do not use body language appropriately, which limits full communication. Some people can be taught how to use body language, but it rarely becomes a natural skill.

Eye contact

Eye contact is a natural and vital part of communication. It tells other people that we are interested in what they have to say and is a part of how we extract meaning from language. The use of eye contact can be a strength in many people with learning difficulties, but for others it will need to be taught. Where a pupil has been taught how to use eye contact it is rare for it to be used entirely naturally. This is particularly true of pupils with autistic spectrum disorders who may find eye contact threatening, or who may be listening intently to what is being said even though they may be looking in the opposite direction. This is a case where knowing a child, and how they communicate, is of paramount importance. The information should be part of the transfer documentation for new pupils.

Objects of reference

Objects of reference are used to represent particular activities, events, people or ideas. They are cues to support understanding for pupils with learning difficulties. Objects of reference can be used as simply as giving a pupil a pencil at the start of each English lesson, a calculator for a maths lesson, a sea shell for a science lesson, or a swimsuit for a session in the pool. The object tells the child what is going to happen next, or what is expected of them. Objects can be used to create an object timetable with the pupil removing each object in turn and taking it to the lesson. The objects need not be directly related to the activity, the association that is built up over time being more important. For example, the objects of reference could be different coloured cubes with the colours relating to different places in school.

Communication boards and books

Communication boards and books are made up of commonly used photographs, symbols or words. The pupil points to the appropriate picture, symbol or word in order to communicate with others. The communication book is usually made up of separate symbols or words backed with Velcro that can be used together to create sentences or sequences of concepts.

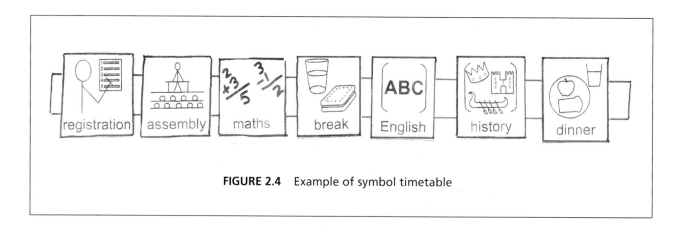

FIGURE 2.4   Example of symbol timetable

Electronic communication aids

Pupils with severe communication difficulties may use a portable electronic communication device. These are usually based on a symbol system and can be very sophisticated. It is important to give pupils time to create their sentence on the machine before looking away or repeating a question. There will need to be a member of staff in school who is trained to use the machine, and is able to help the pupil with technical matters.

Symbols

Symbols are around us all the time whether we are driving, at work, or shopping in the supermarket. Symbols are not just for people with learning difficulties. Many schools have found that developing the use of symbols across the curriculum has benefited many more pupils than solely those with special needs. Symbols support communication, independence and participation, literacy, creativity, and access to information.

There are a number of symbol systems available for use in schools. The most effective way of developing the use of symbols is by installing Writing With Symbols 2000 (from Widgit Software) onto a computer. The program produces symbols as words are typed into a word processor. Grids are easy to make and can create simple and quick communication boards. No additional training for staff is needed to help them understand the symbols as the word is printed below the symbol. It is a very simple way of making accessible worksheets for individual pupils. As with many resources designed for pupils with learning difficulties, the software has a much wider relevance, especially for pupils with specific learning difficulties or other reading difficulties who would benefit from having additional visual support with text. A sample of Writing with Symbols 2000 communication grid is included on the CD, by permission of Widgit Software www.widgit.com.

Behaviour

Where pupils have limited ways to communicate their needs and wishes, behaviour becomes a vital communication tool. It takes a long time to get to know a pupil well enough to decipher what they want from their behaviour alone, but it is wonderfully rewarding when that understanding occurs. For pupils without an obvious or diagnosed disability it is always worth noting any change in behaviour patterns as this could indicate an underlying problem.

CASE STUDY | **Philip**

Case study: Philip

Philip is in Year 8. He has cerebral palsy and communicates using a symbol communication board and eye pointing. His understanding is very good. He started refusing to use his communication board and became temperamental, not looking at adults and shouting and crying for much of the time. His school work deteriorated. An early annual review was called to discuss the difficulties. In the course of the meeting, Philip's mother said that his granny was in the hospice with a terminal illness. Philip's behaviour had not changed much at home but he had been more 'clingy' than usual.

Philip's behaviour deteriorated because he was worried about his granny, to whom he was very close. He had not been taken to see her in the hospice as it was thought he would be upset. Both Philip's parents and his form tutor talked to him about his feelings and a counsellor came to school and worked with him. He was taken to see his granny in the hospice.

Once this understanding had been established, Philip was able to resume both his usual communication and school work. When, some weeks later, his granny died he was allowed to go to the funeral, and his school and his parents supported him through that time without his work or behaviour being affected.

Summary

Thorough preparation for inclusion is the most important factor for success, both to prepare for greater diversity in your school, and to include an individual pupil with learning difficulties. The time from that first impression through to the child arriving on the first day of a new school year is the window of opportunity, to find out as much as possible about the child and what the school can do to make the placement a success. The preparation, liaison and training undertaken will be of enormous value for the future development of the school, 'clearing the ramp' for other pupils with a more diverse range of needs and talents.

Chapter 3 looks at how schools can group pupils to support inclusion.

Grouping for inclusion

To be able to learn and play alongside their chronological peers is a vital part of inclusion for pupils with learning difficulties. There are no lessons on how to be twelve or thirteen – children work this out for themselves by being together, talking, listening to music, watching older pupils being cool, and by distancing themselves from the younger ones! Without this everyday contact a pupil with learning difficulties becomes even more different; in how they dress, their interests – even in the words they use. Adults are very caring and well-meaning but they no longer have the 'social code' of young people.

Students with learning difficulties need to have the experiences, resources, materials and activities that would be expected for any other pupil of the same age. In class, a pupil with significant learning difficulties may still be working on objectives from Key Stage 1, but that does not mean they have to use infant workbooks. The content of the work and the objectives may be from Key Stage 1, but the context, materials, and the expectations of how the student should work, need to be radically different.

Which year group?

The right group for a pupil with learning difficulties is one where they are with children they already know – from their previous school or from the local neighbourhood. These are the same criteria which all schools use to group pupils transferring from primary. These criteria are far more important than class size or the amount of support available; learning difficulty is not in itself a reason to segregate. Grouping pupils with students whom they already know will help them settle more quickly and effectively into a new environment. These classmates will be a natural source of continuity and support.

Where children move to a new school with which they have no links, the school will need to work extra hard to help to develop social links. A buddy system or Circles of Friends approach will give a basis for relationships and help pupils to develop the necessary skills and strategies to become part of their peer group. Schools sometimes decide to 'wait and see' for a few weeks how the pupil gets on with the other students, but this is rarely successful. Much more effective is a proactive approach from the beginning, which makes the class a more cohesive group and benefits everyone in it.

Personal, Social and Health Education and Citizenship

Personal, social and health education (PSHE) and Citizenship policies and courses within the school are the ideal vehicles for promoting and developing a greater acceptance of diversity, both in school and in society as a whole. These policies will set the framework for the development of more inclusive attitudes and practices. The Programmes of Study for Citizenship at both Key Stages 3 and 4 emphasise the importance for students of learning about 'fairness, social justice, respect for democracy and diversity at school, local, national and global level': also ' to respect the differences between people as they develop their own sense of identity' (DfEE 1999). Many of these aspects can be addressed not only through the PSHE and Citizenship policies and courses but also in the way the school supports inclusive attitudes and behaviour among students, and between students and staff. Students will take their lead from the adults around them and how members of staff show respect and tolerance for pupils with learning difficulties is of great importance. Being part of a buddy system or a Circle of Friends will do much more than any number of lessons to develop pupils' understanding of diversity, social justice and fairness.

Buddy systems and Circles of Friends

Peer support for pupils with learning difficulties is an effective and powerful tool for inclusion, and yet schools are often remarkably reluctant to make use of a natural resource. Often there is a fear that parents of the supporting pupils will object, that it is unfair on the other students, or that work will suffer as a consequence. In practice peer support is rarely a burden for students, and is usually of benefit to all concerned.

Buddies

It is reasonable to expect one pupil to help another from time to time. A buddy system simply makes that help more formal and gives the supporters a framework in which to operate. The majority of buddy systems are based on pairing pupils in order to, for example, guide and support a new student through the initial settling in process. Such a paired system could put too much responsibility on one person and so a buddy scheme that involves a small number of supporters – four or five – is more appropriate for pupils who have learning difficulties. Careful selection of buddies at the outset is important for the future success of the scheme. The buddies can be chosen either from the pupil's own form or from an older year group, depending on whether the support is for all the time in school or only for breaks and lunchtimes. Preparation for the buddies is very important if they are to be effective, with the boundaries of their role carefully defined. For example, the buddy's role in the playground would be to talk with the pupil with learning difficulties and encourage him or her to join games. The buddy would not be expected to intervene in disputes with other pupils, except to inform a member of staff. The amount of time spent in support should be limited, and buddies need to have time to give feedback to staff. There also needs to be time to discuss any issues that may arise. A written schedule of regular support and feedback meetings will protect all the parties from becoming overburdened.

> ### CASE STUDY | Kevin's buddy scheme
>
> Kevin's buddy sheet (on the accompanying CD) shows how his four buddies take the lead on one break each every day, with the same person supporting Kevin when he arrives at school and when he leaves. The buddy timetable is changed every week and at the end of each month the buddies are given the opportunity to drop out. Kevin joins drama club on Wednesday evenings and Megan volunteered to be his buddy in the club for the autumn term.
>
> Kevin's key teacher, Mr Jones, is in charge of the buddy scheme. He monitors the scheme closely and offers advice and support where necessary. He also arranges a weekly, informal meeting for all the buddies with tea and biscuits. The buddies are encouraged to discuss any successes as well as any problems that may have come up and how they dealt with the situations. The group has an outing to a cinema or theme park each term which is funded by the school. The group vote on whether to include Kevin on the outing – and he hasn't missed one yet.

Talk partners

The talk-partner system has been developed in primary schools but is equally appropriate in secondary classes. Rather than pupils putting up hands and answering questions, pupils discuss questions with a talk partner before either answering verbally or writing the answer on a small whiteboard. Talk partners support pupils with learning difficulties very well, enabling them to answer questions and practise speaking and listening skills.

Subject buddies

The concept of subject buddies is based on the lab partners system that is used in science. All pupils with special needs are assigned a partner for each subject for a period of up to half a term at a time. The partner may be another pupil with learning difficulties who would benefit from sharing teaching assistant support, or a more able pupil who would be able to explain concepts in a coherent but simplified way.

Circle of Friends

The Circles of Friends approach originated in North America and has been used in mainstream settings to support children with a wide range of disabilities. The circle consists of between six and eight students who volunteer to form a support network for a particular child. The circle is led by an adult, usually an educational psychologist or a teacher. A weekly meeting with the whole circle is held to discuss any difficulties and to work out ways of resolving problems for the pupil.

The Circles of Friends has four main aims:

- To create a support network of other pupils for the child.
- To help the child cope more easily in school and to give him or her more choices.
- To provide the child with encouragement and recognition for achievements and progress.
- To work with the child to identify difficulties and to come up with practical ideas to help sort out problems.

Setting up a circle includes:

- Gaining the support and agreement of the focus pupil and his or her parents.
- A meeting with the whole class (which the focus pupil does not attend) aimed at identifying those willing to be supporters.
- Informing the parents of those chosen to be circle members, and obtaining their agreement to their child's participation.
- Weekly meetings of the circle, the focus pupil, and an adult facilitator. (Newton and Wilson 1999)

The time commitment of the circle members needs to be monitored carefully to make sure the support is not taking up too much of their time, and is being shared equally amongst the group. The time commitment for staff is roughly 40–60 minutes to set up the circle, and weekly meetings of 20–30 minutes. A bonus of the Circles of Friends approach is that where some of the circle members have behavioural, emotional or social difficulties, the circle often has a positive effect on their behaviour and self-esteem in school, in addition to the positive support for the focus child.

CASE STUDY | **David**

David has problems during transition between classes. He frequently hits other pupils and runs out of school. David is in Year 7 and he has an autistic spectrum disorder and moderate learning difficulties. He thinks he is being attacked by other students when they touch him with their elbows or their bags in the busy corridors. His response is to hit out and try to get away as quickly as possible. David is well behaved in class and he had no behaviour difficulties in his primary school. The behaviour support service teacher recommended a buddy scheme involving four boys from David's form group. The boys were asked to walk with David between lessons, one at each side of him, one in front and one behind. In this way David is shielded from other pupils and cannot be knocked by them. In conjunction with the buddy scheme, a social story was written to explain to David that the collisions in the corridor were not meant as attacks. The social story teaches him alternative ways of behaving when he feels anxious.

After two weeks David no longer needed the formal support of his buddies and they were able to walk with him in a more natural grouping. All four boys were glad to help David and, as they came to know him better, they began to like him and want to spend time with him – especially when they found out about his expertise on computer games.

Puberty

Another important reason for keeping pupils with learning difficulties with their chronological peers is that most will go through the changes of puberty at about the same time. If taught with a younger group, pupils with learning difficulties will enter puberty alone, and will not be able to share their important new experiences. The only thing that makes teenage acne and greasy hair bearable is the knowledge that everyone else in the class is suffering too! The best way for pupils to learn how to behave through this momentous time is to be with others experiencing the same changes.

The skate boarders, the goths and the nerds!

Within any secondary school, pupils will group themselves according to their interests. It is useful to watch students from a neighbouring school arrive at their campus. Even where a school has a strict uniform policy the pupils will have made choices about, and changes to, their clothes that reinforce their identity in a sub-group.

This can be as subtle as to how socks are worn – pulled up or rolled down; hair colour and style; regulation school trousers for the 'nerds', or baggy ones worn teetering on the hips for the skate boarders; long skirts for the Goths, or short skirts for the 'babes' etc. These differences become more apparent where there is no uniform code, or in sixth forms, with pupils taking on the 'look' of their particular group.

Some of the identities are transitory, lasting only as long as the latest particular fad. For example, gelled, spiky hair might be just the thing for a boy at thirteen but will be completely unacceptable a year later.

The importance of these adolescent experiences should not be underestimated stemming as they do from both the desire to be different, and the need to conform to a group. They form part of the adolescent rite of passage. Whereas we cannot force pupils with learning difficulties to join a particular group, they should have the opportunity to choose for themselves if that is what they want.

Age-appropriate resources and experiences

While pupils are in classes teachers should strive to offer materials, resources, and activities appropriate for the student's age. It is important, however, that adults do not confuse the offering of pupil age-appropriate materials in class with taking away their freedom to choose their own belongings. An example would be a Thomas the Tank Engine lunchbox or a Barbie folder. Students must be allowed to choose their own belongings for use outside the classroom. Many young people hang on to certain items from childhood; the ragged bit of cot blanket or the teddy bear is still on the bed at university! These items are important and in uncertain times are comforting links to the familiar. Some such choices could make the pupil liable to teasing or bullying, and would need to be discussed with parents. A less isolating solution might be found, such as keeping the Thomas lunchbox inside a plain bag. But if the pupil insists on keeping their things out in the open they should be allowed to do so. Actual or potential bullying or teasing should be addressed through the school's bullying policy, underpinned by the determination of all staff to make the school a safe place for everyone. It is not up to any pupil to avoid being bullied – that is the school's job.

Sex education

Sexual development is always a difficult and sensitive issue when related to people with learning difficulties. Society may expect them to exist in a sort of 'everlasting childhood', but no-one remains a child forever. Such attitudes do not help students develop independence as adults. People with learning difficulties do form lasting and meaningful sexual relationships, and they are entitled to the same support and information that is given to all students. Information is delivered most effectively as a component of a wider unit of work looking at relationships and lifestyle choices.

Discussion with the family will be vital at this stage of development as parental wishes will need taking into consideration. Where pupils mix socially with their chronological peers, it is surprising how much information they pick up from watching television with friends, or from listening to conversations. Individual or small group tutorials aimed at preparing students for sex education lessons are useful, as they give an idea of what is going to happen, and give the student the opportunity to ask questions and clear up any misunderstandings. Other specialist materials, such as anatomical models or life-like baby dolls, can be used in these individual or small group sessions and these will support understanding. Watching a video with a trusted adult before seeing it in the whole-class lesson will help the student to overcome any embarrassment.

Extracurricular activities

Extracurricular activities offer pupils with learning difficulties unique opportunities to become involved with other students on an equal basis. Even if not ready to take the lead role in the school production, they could be in the chorus, or be very involved backstage with scenery, costumes or make-up. Not many adults remember the maths lessons in Year 9 but most remember the after-play parties! While the pupil with learning difficulties may not make the A squad in team games, they can excel in other physical activities such as dance, trampolining, or aerobics. Where schools give equal importance to the less competitive areas of sport as they do to team games, both participation and achievement will be increased for the pupil with learning difficulties.

School social and sporting events are important milestones in children's lives, and they are no less important for those with learning difficulties. There may be issues of support and care, but these are not insurmountable, and if the pupil has always been included it will be natural for him or her to join in on these occasions.

Taking risks

Risk-taking is a thorny issue for people with learning difficulties of all ages. Without experiencing some level of risk, students will never develop any level of independence. Risks range from a possibility of a broken arm in an abseiling activity to a broken heart in a youthful relationship. Just as we take a calculated risk when we join a mountaineering group, so we must give pupils with learning difficulties the chance to take their own risks within controlled bounds.

Of course schools must do all they can to keep their students safe, but challenging activities such as outward bound courses, or the Duke of Edinburgh Award Scheme, give students an understanding of their own abilities and limitations. Students with learning difficulties are often barred from working in design and technology workshops or school kitchens because of dangers inherent in the equipment. Yet without learning how to use some of this machinery, how are students ever to learn how to cook, or to work with wood? Health and safety must be paramount, but a blanket ban on all potentially hazardous equipment is unnecessary. Risk assessments are a useful starting point when making decisions about hazardous activities and the assessments can be completed with the intention of enabling a pupil to participate rather than to be excluded. Teaching pupils with learning difficulties to use simple hand tools to work with wood, or a sewing machine for textiles, or a food processor, can open up a new dimension to their whole lives and they will begin to develop new skills and independence.

Which set?

Most secondary schools put pupils into sets for some subjects according to ability. The system works well for most pupils, but there can be problems for pupils with learning difficulties if they are placed always in bottom sets. The bottom set is usually smaller and has more support available, but it may also include some pupils who have behavioural, emotional and social difficulties. Pupils with learning difficulties find it very hard to work in a class where there is disruption. They may become distressed or withdrawn or, more seriously, begin to copy the behaviours they see in an attempt to fit in.

Why not consider allowing the pupil with learning difficulties to work in a top set? There they will have good role models of behaviour and attitudes to work. Even in the bottom set, it is likely that the work would have to be differentiated, and where subject teachers plan the work and differentiation together the load will be shared and should not be too onerous. Sometimes teachers are concerned that more able pupils will be disturbed by having a pupil with learning difficulties in the class. There is no reason why a pupil with learning difficulties should make more noise than any other pupil, especially once used to working in a purposeful environment. Most lessons involve some teacher talk interspersed with quiet discussion between students and as pupils are used to working at home with the television on or with music playing, it is unlikely that they will be distracted by a fellow pupil asking questions of the teacher or teaching assistant.

Position in the classroom

Most pupils choose where they sit in lessons. Where a pupil has learning difficulties, there is no inherent reason why they should not choose their own place in the classroom, but in some circumstances the teacher may need to 'orchestrate'. For pupils who may have problems with hearing or sight, it is worth making sure the student can see and hear the teacher, though where there are acoustic problems within a room, these should be addressed for the benefit of all pupils. Also very important is easy access to any equipment that might be needed. Where specialist equipment is subject specific, it may always be kept in a box in the classroom or laboratory. Additional resources that give pupils a wider variety of activities in lessons could also be kept in the box. For example, a maths resources box could contain a large-key calculator, Unifix cubes, 2D and 3D shapes, and a ruler. Put in a set of dominos and a pack of playing cards, and the teacher or teaching assistant will have other age-appropriate but meaningful mathematical activities with which to break up a long lesson.

Where a pupil with learning difficulties is supported one-to-one by a teaching assistant, try to make sure the teaching assistant does not block the pupil off from the rest of the class, as this will isolate them. There is rarely a need for the teaching assistant to sit next to a pupil throughout a lesson. When the teaching assistant works with a group that includes the pupil with learning difficulties, or moves around the class supporting others, the support is more effective.

To withdraw or not to withdraw?

Schools withdraw pupils from classes for many reasons and for varying amounts of time each week. This is often to give additional time to work on basic literacy or numeracy skills. A balance needs to be struck between giving pupils the additional support they might need and limiting the range of subjects they are able to access. The more frequently pupils are taken out of lessons, the less they going to be a part of the class and the more different they will appear to other students. There are very few lessons that cannot be differentiated sufficiently to give all pupils an enriching, rewarding and educationally valid experience in each of the different subjects. Literacy skills may also be addressed in other subjects. It may be that while the rest of the class is addressing a history objective, the pupil with learning difficulties is working within the history context on a literacy target from his or her Individual Education Plan. For example, based on the IEP at Figure 3.1, Devon's history teacher will incorporate five of the high frequency words from his English IEP target into the lesson. Devon's target words that are especially relevant to history are *after*, *because*, *from*, *next*, and *then*, and he will be helped to spell them in his work when adding captions to pictures.

This is where staff teamwork pays dividends. The subject team needs to work with the SENCO to organise exactly what is to be covered, and to decide which resources they will need to make the dividends possible to achieve.

Withdrawal of the pupil with learning difficulties as part of a group can be beneficial. Such a group could be supported by the teacher or a teaching assistant for part of a lesson, and might involve researching a particular topic in the library, accessing IT equipment, or preparing for a future lesson. In this way, the pupil with learning difficulties has social support from the group, and the opportunity to learn in different environments with different people. In general, pupils

INDIVIDUAL EDUCATION PLAN

Name: Devon Jones

Year: 7

Stage: School Action Plus

Start date: January 2004

Review date: March 2004

IEP No.: 2

Area of concern: literacy, personal organisation

Strengths: social skills, music and dance

Teacher/Support: Mrs Francis (TA) every morning

Targets:

1. Devon will learn to read 10 new 'personal' words from his self books.

2. Devon will learn to spell correctly 15 high frequency words. He will use these words in his school work without support.

3. Devon will arrive at lessons with his pencil case and correct books.

Strategies for use in class:

1. Encourage Devon to write his target words by himself if he asks for help.
2. Incorporate his personal words into lessons where possible and praise him when he reads them.
3. Arrange for Devon to work in pairs and small groups rather than always with Mrs Francis.
4. Make sure he has access to and uses his AlphaSmart computer for recording.
5. Praise Devon for having the correct books with him and write a positive note in his diary.

Role of parent(s)/carer(s):

1. To share Devon's self books every day and go through his new words with him.

2. To play with Devon the spelling games sent home by Mrs Francis to reinforce his new spelling words.

3. Each evening, to help Devon prepare his school bag for the next day, using his crib card.

Success criteria:

1) Devon will read the new words in his self books with increased understanding and confidence.

2) He will use the 15 new spellings in subjects across the curriculum.

3) He will settle down to work more quickly and have more positive comments from teachers and Mrs Francis in his diary.

Resources:

1) List of Devon's new reading and spelling words to be given to all his teachers.

2) Devon to have access to Wordshark and Starspell software in computer suite on 2 lunchtimes each week.

3) Devon to meet his learning mentor for one hour each week (Wednesday, period 1) to discuss progress towards his targets.

Agreed by:

SENCO:

Parent(s)/Carer(s):

Pupil:

Date:

FIGURE 3.1   Completed Individual Education Plan

learn more in the main classroom context than in an isolated one-to-one withdrawal situation. Any additional specific literacy or numeracy needs can be addressed through homework. Parents are often very glad to have a programme to follow at home, and several of the catch-up programmes from the earlier stages of the National Literacy or Numeracy Strategies are suitable for this purpose.

Interaction

Try to make sure that pupils with learning difficulties have the opportunity to interact with other students during every lesson and not just with the teacher or teaching assistant. Pairing pupils together to discuss a subject for a limited time, or to prepare a topic to present to the rest of the class, is an ideal way of developing understanding and cooperation and gives pupils the opportunity to learn appropriate independent listening and thinking skills from their peers. It also helps the other pupils organise and understand their own thinking by having to pass on and simplify information.

Less formal interaction in classes should also be encouraged where appropriate. Simple interactions might include asking to borrow equipment, sharing textbooks, waiting one's turn, holding the door open for the person behind. These actions are the bases of the social behaviour pupils will need as adults, and not only develop valuable skills such as speaking, listening, and turn taking, but also foster more personal qualities such as empathy and patience.

Grouping strategies

Composition of groups in lessons will need to be considered carefully if students are to work together effectively. Here are some suggestions for grouping pupils that both support the inclusion of pupils with learning difficulties and enhance the learning experiences for all the class.

- Pupils work in pairs for part of each lesson, discussing topics or sharing ideas that are then fed back to the whole group – The pupil with learning difficulties may give an interesting new perspective to discussions. Changing the partner each lesson would prevent any one pupil taking on too much of a support role, and could encourage those who may be less caring to develop this side of their personality.
- Create small groups within the classroom which receive additional attention from the teacher or teaching assistant – With this strategy the pupil receives help from both peers and staff. Vary the groups in each lesson so that no one group always includes the pupil with learning difficulties.
- Create small groups which, with a teacher or teaching assistant, work outside the ordinary classroom for part of the time – This form of withdrawal should be used sparingly as pupils need to become used to working in the classroom environment.
- Pupil-led groups that discuss an aspect of a lesson and give feedback to the whole class – This strategy gives pupils responsibility for some of their own learning and encourages cooperation. Management of this kind of group can be problematic, especially where some pupils are more dominant than others. A more formal approach, such as a cooperative learning 'Jigsaw' strategy, may be more appropriate for groups with a wide range of abilities.

- Small-group withdrawal sessions to prepare pupils for inclusion in a later lesson as opposed to withdrawal for parallel teaching – The teacher or teaching assistant works with pupils on work to be covered in a forthcoming lesson. This could include learning facts, preparing questions, or putting together a presentation for the rest of the class.

Cooperative learning

Cooperative learning is a teaching strategy in which small teams, each consisting of pupils with differing levels of ability, use a variety of learning activities to improve their understanding of a subject. Each member of a team is responsible not only for their own learning but also for helping their team-mates to learn, so creating an atmosphere of achievement. Pupils work through an assignment until all the members of the team successfully understand it and it is completed.

Cooperative learning strategies are useful because they reduce peer competition and isolation, and promote academic achievement and positive interrelationships. Teachers can use cooperative learning through peer interactions and carefully designed activities to help students make connections between the concrete and abstract level of instruction.

Cooperative learning creates natural interactive contexts in which pupils have authentic reasons for listening to one another, asking questions, clarifying issues, and restating points of view.

Cooperative learning methods share certain characteristics:

- pupils work together on common activities that are best learned through team work;
- pupils work together in small teams of between two and six pupils;
- pupils use cooperative behaviour to complete learning activities;
- activities are structured so that pupils have to work together if they are to complete the learning activities;
- pupils are individually accountable for their own learning.

The elements of cooperative learning are:

- *Positive interdependence*: the efforts of each group member are indispensable if the group is to be successful.
- *Face to face interaction*: teaching the other pupils in the group and checking for understanding.
- *Individual and group accountability*: each individual team member is accountable for his or her own learning, and for the learning of the others in the team. The group is accountable for supporting its own team members.
- *Interpersonal and small-group skills*: supports the development of social skills such as leadership, decision-making, and communication.
- *Group processing*: team members discuss how well they achieved their goal, and describe what they found useful.

One system of cooperative learning that is relatively simple and that can be used in most subjects is Jigsaw (Aronson and Patnoe 1997).

| Box 3.1 | **How to arrange a Jigsaw activity** |

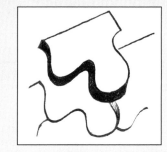

1. Divide the class into teams of 5 or 6 pupils. The teams should be as diverse as possible in terms of ability.
2. Appoint one student from each team to be the leader.
3. Divide the lesson into five or six segments, depending on the number of pupils in the groups. The level of challenge in each segment can be varied to meet the abilities of individual pupils.
4. Assign each pupil one segment to learn. Pupils have access only to their own segment.
5. Give pupils time to read through their segment at least twice. For some pupils the written material will also need to have supporting symbols or be available on a personal stereo. There is no need for pupils to memorise the information.
6. Form temporary 'expert' groups by having one pupil from each group join other pupils assigned to the same segment. Give the expert groups time to discuss the main points of their segment, and to devise and rehearse the presentations they will make to their own teams.
7. Regroup pupils back into their original teams.
8. Ask each student to present his or her segment to the team. Encourage other pupils in the team to ask questions for clarification.
9. The teacher moves from team to team, observing the process and making any necessary interventions.
10. At the end of the session, give a quiz on the information learned so that pupils realise that they all benefit from learning together.

| Box 3.2 | **Jigsaw in the classroom: Year 8 Geography** |

QCA Schemes of Work: Unit 11. Investigating Brazil Section 4: What is it like? (QCA 2000)

One hour lesson. Class of 30 pupils. Class divided into groups of five.

The team are all working on the same topic: Brazil, what is it like?

The topic was divided up by the teacher into five segments:

- rivers
- industry
- population
- climate
- ecosystems

All the jigsaw teams had one member assigned to each segment.

The students then divided into expert groups together with the other students working on the same segment. These expert groups had access to a variety of information; CD-ROM, internet sites, videos, travel brochures, and textbooks, to enable them to gather information. The expert groups had twenty minutes to collect the necessary information and to decide on the five key points they were to take back to their jigsaw teams.

The students returned to their jigsaw teams and each student then presented the key points about their segment. Each student had five minutes to deliver their information. Other students asked questions to clarify points.

The teacher gave the class a quiz on the main points of the topic for the final fifteen minutes of the lesson.

A win-win situation

Including pupils with learning difficulties in mainstream subject lessons is challenging – but in a positive way. Teachers say that including these pupils often takes them back to the core of their vocation. Being creative with a curriculum subject and identifying the really important aspects of what is taught, and why, can bring the fun back into the work. Other students too will enjoy the challenge of learning in new ways. There is currently a great deal of research into the differing learning styles of pupils. Much of the differentiation we need to make for pupils with learning difficulties involves making learning more visual, and more kinaesthetic. Where teachers strike a balance in their lessons between the auditory, the visual, and the kinaesthetic, pupils achieve more, and there is a lower incidence of disruptive behaviour.

When all pupils are included and respected in groups within lessons, the achievement of all improves. Inclusion is not about educating pupils with learning difficulties at the expense of others. It is about making schools more effective and responsive for all.

The Grouping Checklist (Figure 3.2) can be used to track a pupil's involvement in different groups over several weeks. It offers teachers and teaching assistants a method of gauging the level of formal and informal interactions in which a student is engaged. This information will be valuable when reporting to annual reviews and when preparing Individual Education Plans. The checklist could be used to inform individual lesson planning as well as longer-term plans. A blank version of the checklist is included on the accompanying CD.

Name: Rhys Jones			Form: 8LTS			Subject: Maths (50 mins)		Teacher: TGB		
Date	8/9	11/9	12/9	15/9	18/9	19/9	22/9	25/9	26/9	29/9
Whole class involvement	10 mins		20 mins (shape)	10 mins	10 mins		15 mins	10 mins		15 mins
Group work										
In class	✓		✓	✓		✓	✓	✓		
Withdrawal		✓			✓				✓	✓
TA support	✓	✓	✓	✓ with group + RJ.	✓		✓		✓	
Peer support			✓ (Callum helped)	✓ (CP + JF)		✓ EB JF DH		✓ DH JF CP		✓ CP DH EB
Pairs										
With TA	✓			✓ plenary		✓				✓ plen.
With peer					✓ (JF)		✓ game + David.			
Informal interactions	Chatted to James	none	Smiled at his group	Eye contact + smiles with group	Lots of speech with James in plenary	Watching others. Bit over-excited.	Nice greeting. Chat with Evan & David	went straight to group. Talking right through	computer suite.	Hi S's! Spoke to his group. Lots of smiles

FIGURE 3.2 Completed grouping checklist

Summary

- Group according to chronological age for all subjects.
- Provide age-appropriate resources, activities and experiences.
- Allow pupils to sit where they choose in class, unless there is a particular reason why they should not.
- Avoid having a teaching assistant with the pupil, one-to-one, all the time as this may lead to the pupil being even more isolated.
- Use individual withdrawal carefully.
- Identify contexts in other subjects for teaching basic literacy and numeracy skills.
- Create opportunities for formal and informal interaction in each lesson.
- Develop a variety of grouping strategies.
- Give opportunities for visual, auditory and kinaesthetic learning in every subject.

The different strategies outlined in this chapter will help schools to include pupils who have learning difficulties in mainstream classes. Perhaps the most important aspect is to keep a balance between the pupil working in class and being withdrawn; between group work and one-to-one support; and between support from a teaching assistant and peer support. Teachers can ensure the balances are maintained by incorporating grouping strategies into their planning.

Grouping for inclusion is also grouping to build future independence – giving pupils the chance to develop the social and communication skills they will need in adult life.

Chapter 4 gives guidance on planning and teaching the curriculum for inclusion in Years 7, 8 and 9.

Planning and teaching the curriculum for inclusion at Key Stage 3

In any mainstream year group there will always be several pupils operating at earlier National Curriculum levels than the majority of their peers. Even where pupils work in sets there will remain a significant minority struggling with basic skills. This chapter will give teachers ideas on how to make the Key Stage 3 curriculum more inclusive for pupils with learning difficulties without creating a mountain of extra work.

Planning for classes that include pupils with learning difficulties is sometimes daunting and teachers can be put off even before they start. It really doesn't have to be complicated, nor need it create a great deal of additional work. The key is not to write a completely different syllabus for one pupil. You can adapt the planning systems you have already. However, planning for pupils with learning difficulties is impossible to do 'on the hoof'; it needs to be done in advance at the same time as the planning for the rest of the group. Keep an extra piece of paper on the side of the desk and as opportunities for differentiation arise, write them down.

It is vital to have high expectations of all pupils even, or especially, for those with learning difficulties.

Often teachers feel the best way to plan for a pupil with learning difficulties is to look for workbooks or materials suitable for the pupil's academic ability level. In effect, this often means the pupil working through infant workbooks with a teaching assistant, with the work they undertake having no connection to that of the rest of the class. In this sort of situation, the pupil with SEN may rarely have any attention from the teacher, resulting in him or her being 'minded' rather then being taught.

New learning should be teacher-led, with teaching assistants supporting the pupils in practising and consolidating the skills and knowledge.

Schools are constantly bombarded with advertisements for new and better materials for pupils with special needs. New sets of books or items of software promise to sort out the planning and meet pupil needs, but all too often they do not. In fact, a teacher's brains and creativity are far superior to any new software or textbook. Try to ignore the advertising blandishments. Totally different resources and activities are not necessary. The answers are rarely found in new resources, no matter how glossy the catalogue or impressive the claim. Talent and experience among teachers and teaching assistants are the most powerful factors in determining a pupil's needs to help them make progress.

Omar

Omar is in Year 8. His reading is at a very early stage of development. He worked on the Oxford Reading Tree scheme until the end of Year 7, but became reluctant to keep on trying, and he was bored with books that he felt were too babyish. Omar finds word building very hard but he can remember some words that have direct relevance to him and his life. His teaching assistant has helped him to create a series of books about his family, his friends, and his special interests, such as helping his father with jobs in the garden and the workshop, and lorries. Each book has the same format, with digital photographs and a word or short phrase underneath. Omar's family were involved in making the books, with his father photographing Omar working in the garden and in the workshop. The books are kept in school but Omar frequently takes them home to share with his family. This work has motivated Omar to learn to read a significant number of new words. The amount of text in each book can be increased as Omar's reading develops.

Targets and progress

No matter how excellent the teaching and the care given, pupils with learning difficulties will fall behind their peers in academic development – and the gap will become increasingly wider as they get older. This is why it is so important to track the pupil's progress and celebrate all achievement. By setting individual, achievable and appropriate targets, everyone can feel satisfied. Parents know their child is making progress; teachers know they are meeting the pupil's needs; and the pupil feels a sense of achievement and fulfilment. The goals may not be the same as for other children but they are no less valid. The old adage of measuring what we value, rather than valuing what we can measure, holds true in this case. If a school as a whole values and celebrates all pupil achievements, academic or otherwise, the whole community is lifted and energised. Life is about more than GCSEs, and good schools develop that more affective side of the curriculum.

Incorporating objectives from other agencies

Increasingly agencies, such as speech and language therapy or occupational therapy, are working in mainstream schools. The old system of taking pupils out of class for therapy is now commonly being replaced by therapists working with teachers and teaching assistants, and incorporating therapy objectives into IEP and curricular targets. Therapists assess the pupil, and give training to the teacher or a teaching assistant. They devise a programme to be carried out in school, and return at regular intervals to check on progress and adjust the programme.

Where there is a good and professional relationship between therapist and school, this system is more effective than the isolated twenty minutes of therapy each week. It makes better use of the therapist's time, and develops valuable skills for teachers and teaching assistants. Parents are often wary of this system, particularly where the pupil has therapy time on his or her Statement of Special Educational Needs. Good communication between therapist, school and parents is needed to help parents understand that their child is receiving better and more effective treatment.

When planning to include a pupil with learning difficulties, check with the SENCO to see if there are therapy objectives that could link in with the unit of work. Physiotherapy targets could be addressed in PE or games, occupational therapy targets in food technology, and speech and language therapy targets are appropriate in most subjects. This means that the impact of the therapy can be multiplied, without the pupil being withdrawn from classes.

Tracking back to success in English, maths and science

Tracking back is the most effective method of setting appropriate learning objectives for pupils with learning difficulties in mainstream classrooms in English, maths and science. The approach is recommended by the Key Stage 3 Strategy for planning for pupils with learning difficulties. The assumption behind the approach is that all pupils, no matter what their level of attainment, should work within a class of their chronological peers.

The starting point for including pupils with learning difficulties is the objective for the whole class from the Key Stage 3 Framework documents for English, maths or science. Once the class objective has been decided, the teacher then tracks back through the Framework documents to an earlier stage to find a related objective for the pupil with learning difficulties. Working through the tracking back process with a teaching assistant who knows the pupil well will ensure the objective is appropriate for the individual, and will spark off ideas for activities and resources. This knowledge about individual pupils is very important in order to decide on teaching strategies and questioning styles that will provide them with the motivation to learn.

For some pupils it will be necessary to track back into previous key stages. Where a pupil is working below Year R level, track back into the P scales (QCA 2001b) (see Chapter 6) which lead into Level 1 of the National Curriculum. Aim to identify relevant objectives that will challenge pupils, but which also are pitched at a relevant and realistic level. This process ensures that pupils experience the full range of the English, maths and science curriculum while working on objectives appropriate to their individual needs.

Take into account the different ways that pupils learn and use this information to influence your choice of teaching strategies. Next, write down anything else you wish to improve or teach the pupil in the context of your subject lesson. For instance

- turn taking
- working independently
- being responsible for collecting his or her own equipment.

This gives the basis for the pupil's work for a series of lessons – academic, personal and social objectives.

Tracking back during the planning process for each half term means the teacher can plan shared activities for all pupils in the class, rather than design completely separate activities for pupils with learning difficulties. The concept of pupils working on individually appropriate objectives within a shared activity is a powerful and effective way of including pupils with a diverse range of learning needs. While tracking back is appropriate for pupils with learning difficulties, tracking forward may be appropriate for more able pupils.

The very important final step is to return to the age-appropriate key stage to prepare the context in which to set the ideas. This last step is vital if pupils are to experience the challenge of a broadening curriculum, which is the cornerstone of teaching in Key Stage 3

Once the objectives and activities for the lessons have been planned, a teaching assistant could further support the process by collecting any additional resources before each lesson, and recording pupil responses. This recording then informs future planning. A sample recording form is included on the accompanying CD.

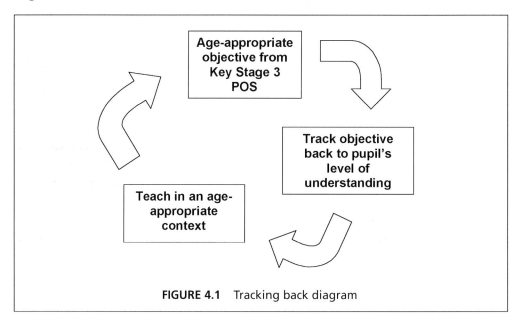

FIGURE 4.1 Tracking back diagram

Tracking back – in short
1. Tracking back takes place at the medium-term planning stage.
2. Start from the age-appropriate objectives in the Key Stage 3 Framework.
3. Track back through the English, maths or science framework for Key Stage 3, 2 or 1 or the P scales to an objective appropriate to the needs of the pupil with learning difficulties.
4. Return to the age-appropriate key stage as this is the context in which the objective will be taught.
5. Identify class and group activities that address the objectives of all the class, *and* the pupil with learning difficulties.

The key concepts method

The foundation subjects at Key Stage 3 do not have the same framework through which to track back. A different approach needs to be taken to be sure that lessons are meaningful for all pupils in the class. The key concepts method works particularly well in history, geography, PSHE and RE.

Once again the starting point is the class objectives. Identify three or four key concepts that you want the pupil with learning difficulties to know – the key concepts of the lesson. For example, in history a Year 8 class learn about the English Civil War; 'Why was 1649 a year of reckoning?' The key concepts for a pupil with learning difficulties could be:

- 1649 is a long time ago
- Charles 1 was beheaded
- Cromwell was Lord Protector.

In addressing these concepts the lesson will also develop specific skills in history, such as:

- To consider significant events and people from British history
- To place events, people and changes into correct periods of time. (QCA 2000)

Planning for the class as a whole is then much easier. The teacher plans the lesson, incorporating a variety of activities and resources that address the key concepts in addition to the class objectives. The pupil with learning difficulties is enabled then to participate, working in groups or with a partner. The sharp focus of two or three key concepts makes assessment much easier and pupils learn more effectively when they know what is expected of them. As the key concepts are a part of what everyone else in the class is learning, they can be shared during the introduction to the lesson – written on the whiteboard or at the top of a worksheet – and referred to again in the plenary to check that the concepts are understood. Figure 4.2 is an example of a completed lesson differentiation planner (a blank version is on the accompanying CD).

Planning lessons to make key concepts accessible ensures that the amount and level of information matches the pupil's ability and understanding. Without this approach, the sheer quantity of information in an undifferentiated lesson, and the level of complexity of both the verbal and written language, will overwhelm pupils with learning difficulties. They cannot access such lessons at any level.

CASE STUDY	Yasmina

An example of the key concepts method

Pupils in a Year 7 geography class are working on Unit 3 of the Key Stage 3 schemes of work: 'What is a settlement?' 'Where do we build settlements and why?' Yasmina is working at P7.

The objectives for the whole class are:

- to define and explain the word 'settlement', and
- to use Ordnance Survey (OS) maps to illustrate the different reasons for settlement location.

The teacher looked at the level description for P7 in the 'Planning, teaching and assessing the curriculum for pupils with learning difficulties' document for geography (QCA 2001a).

continued on p. 43

	Support	Grouping	Resources	Recording	Key knowledge
Name: Kuli		**Form:** 8LS **Subject:** History	**Teacher:** Mr Rashid		**TA:** Mr Collins
Activity 1 Introduction 10 minutes	Sit with Katy as talk partner with Mr Collins on same table	Pair and table group	Small whiteboard for each pair. 'Listen' symbol to give reminders when Mr Rashid speaking. List of key words.	n/a	To consider significant events and people from British history and to place events, people and changes into correct periods of time.
Activity 2 Create column for front page of newspaper telling of death of Charles 1 20 minutes	Mr Rashid and group	Group of 4 band D pupils	Digital camera. A1 paper on flipchart. Marker pens.	Digital camera	**Key concepts** • 1649 is a long time ago • Charles 1 was beheaded • Cromwell was Lord Protector
Activity 3 Clicker 4 activity on computer 10 minutes	Mr Collins	Paired work at the computer with Joseph	Clicker 4 software with French Revolution grid.	Printout	**Key words** King Beheaded
Activity 4 Plenary 10 minutes	Sit with Katy as talk partner with Mr Collins on same table	Pair and table group	Small whiteboard for each pair. 'Listen' symbol to give reminders when Mr Rashid speaking. List of key words.	n/a	Parliament

FIGURE 4.2 Example of a completed lesson differentiation planner

> At P7 pupils should communicate their preferences about the physical/natural and human/made features of places. They begin to use symbols to represent direction, and can represent and record key features of a place using models or symbols. They are aware of their role in caring for their own environment. (QCA 2001a)

Based on this description, the teacher and teaching assistant identified two key concepts of the lesson for Yasmina:

- to identify and name buildings/locations known to her; and,
- to learn the OS symbols for castle, golf course, horse riding, museum, theme park and telephone.

The teacher and TA prepared activities for the lesson that involved Yasmina working in a group, then with a teaching assistant, and finally with one other pupil.

The first activity involved small groups of pupils looking at photographs of different kinds of building that make up a settlement, for example a cottage, a factory, a block of flats, etc. The group discussed the images and Yasmina was able to name several of the buildings.

Yasmina then worked with a teaching assistant. They looked at photographs of buildings familiar to Yasmina – her home, a supermarket, a petrol station, the post office, the mosque, etc. Together they made a book about the town and the familiar landmarks. They included information on where Yasmina's parents worked, the transport she used to travel to school, and the mosque where her family worshipped. Then, on the computer, Yasmina worked on Inclusive Writer, a talking word processor, to write the captions for the book. Yasmina then played a lotto game with a partner, matching OS symbols to photographs. After the game, she stuck the symbols into her geography book. Her geography homework assignment was to learn all six symbols by the next lesson.

Key concepts – in short

The teacher and teaching assistant together should:

- Prepare the class objectives for the lesson.
- Look at the National Curriculum or P scales level description in the subject that matches the ability of the pupil with learning difficulties.
- Identify two or three key concepts from the class objectives that match the level of understanding of the pupil.
- Plan the lesson, incorporating group and individual activities that address the key concepts.
- Prepare any additional resources.
- Share the key concepts with the whole class.
- Return to key concepts at the end of the lesson to check understanding.
- Assess against the key concepts after each lesson (and any IEP targets which may have been addressed).

Curriculum overlapping

The majority of pupils with learning difficulties need to spend additional school time working on communication, reading, writing and maths targets from Individual Education Plans. Often in a mainstream secondary school it is neither possible nor desirable to withdraw pupils from class to work on these basic skills. An option that allows these skills to be developed in subject lessons is curriculum overlapping (Giangreco, Cloninger and Iverson 1998).

In curriculum overlapping the pupil with learning difficulties joins in all lessons with his or her chronological age group. For some lessons, the pupil with learning difficulties focuses on literacy or numeracy targets from an Individual Education Plan, while the rest of the class work on subject objectives in, for example, history, geography, music or biology. The context for the learning is the subject area. The pupil with learning difficulties is still expected to work in groups or with a partner.

Curriculum overlapping must be developed by the SENCO, subject teachers and teaching assistants working together as a team. There needs to be careful planning to give the pupil opportunities to address the IEP targets while maintaining his or her entitlement to a broad and balanced curriculum.

| Box 4.1 | **Examples of curriculum overlapping** |

Josef

Josef is in Year 9. He has Williams Syndrome. He has good expressive language but his comprehension is comparatively delayed. Josef has a reading age of 6 years and 5 months. His IEP target for writing is:

> Josef will write two or three word captions to match pictures

The Year 9 geography class is learning about the importance of tourism as an economic activity. One of the class outcomes is to identify different types of holiday. To address both the geography outcome, and Josef's IEP writing target, the teacher shows the class pictures of different kinds of holiday. Josef is given six holiday pictures and, with a partner, writes a short sentence for each picture using a laptop with Clicker 4 software. Curriculum overlapping can also be used to address other IEP targets.

Poppy

Poppy's IEP includes a behaviour target, as she finds it very difficult to sit still and concentrate for more than five minutes at a time. In the same geography lesson she is working on the target 'Poppy will stay in her seat and on task for 10 minutes'. The context in which she is working is a Year 9 geography lesson but it is the IEP target that will be focus of the lesson and assessment for Poppy.

Making connections

The ability to generalise information from one context to another is an area of particular weakness for pupils with learning difficulties. Even where they show understanding and attainment in one context, it cannot be assumed that they will be able to use that understanding and knowledge in a different context. For example, a pupil may be able to weigh amounts in grams in maths lessons but may need to be taught the skill again in food technology.

Where possible, find and build on links with other subjects to help pupils generalise information across subjects. Make those links explicit. Remind the pupil what they have learned previously, and show them the relevant page in their exercise book or folder. In each lesson take a photograph of the pupil with learning difficulties, either holding an object related to the topic or involved in an activity. This will help him or her to remember the lesson and to begin to make the necessary links to other areas of the curriculum.

The discrete subjects at Key Stage 3 do not easily lend themselves to links between the different areas of the curriculum, possibly with the exception of literacy and numeracy. However, all pupils benefit when cross-curricular themes can be identified and links made explicit.

Concept maps are a valuable way of making visual links between subjects and information (Buzan 2003). A concept map is made up of words, colours, lines and/or pictures. The map helps pupils to organise their thinking, and to remember information. An adult can create the concept map if the pupil is not able to do it for him or herself. Using different colours, shapes, pictures, and even photographs, supports learning and aids memory. Keep the maps clear and simple, or they will add to the pupil's confusion. 'Kidspiration' and 'Inspiration' software (Inspiration Software Inc) helps pupils who have reading and writing difficulties understand concepts by organising and categorising information visually.

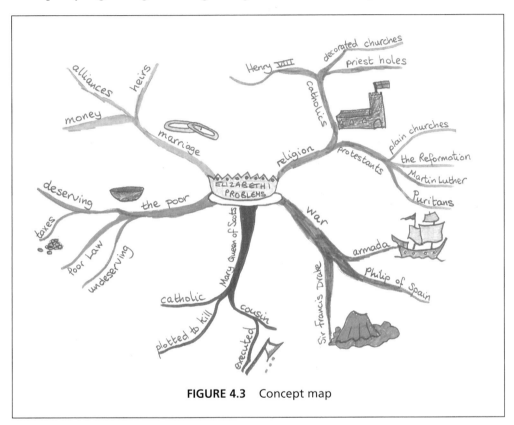

FIGURE 4.3   Concept map

Revisiting concepts

The first time around, pupils with learning difficulties will rarely learn and retain information. They will need opportunities to revisit concepts several times and in different situations. The old army sergeant adage of 'Tell 'em what you're going to tell 'em; tell them; then tell 'em what you've just told 'em', describes just the right approach for pupils with learning difficulties.

Make the objective clear at the start of the lesson so they know what they are going to learn. Teach the concept through a variety of activities and with a range of resources. Then go back to the objective to show the pupil what they have learned.

Multi-sensory learning

The traditional 'chalk and talk' type of lesson will exclude many pupils who have a visual or kinaesthetic learning style; any pupils with hearing loss or visual impairment; and those with learning or communication difficulties. This will encompass a significant group of pupils in every class, particularly in the winter months when even a bad cold can significantly reduce the acuity of hearing. A sensory impairment does not need to be severe to have a profound impact on learning – an out of date, or dirty, pair of prescription spectacles, for example, will limit a student's vision.

Most pupils will benefit from teaching styles which maximise multi-sensory involvement but, by the time pupils reach Key Stage 3, lessons are largely sedentary with the emphasis on auditory information and writing tasks. In the Foundation Stage and Key Stage 1 the curriculum is founded on play-based learning, with practical activities giving children the opportunity to explore through all senses. They are encouraged to run, climb, stretch, roll, and explore the world around them. Through the primary phase, however, the amount of exploration and practical activity gradually diminishes until it is largely limited to drama, PE, and design and technology lessons. Some pupils, even as teenagers and young adults, need more activity and it is unreasonable to expect some of them to sit still for fifty minutes or an hour at a time. A checklist is included on the accompanying CD on which to monitor pupil activity.

Variation and pace

Our students are used to receiving information from the media in short sharp bites – the MTV generation. Varied activities in short bursts make lessons more interesting and memorable, but the rapid pace of some lessons does serve to exclude certain pupils; those with learning difficulties, those with communication difficulties, those with attention disorders, and those with sensory impairments. It is important for lessons to have pace, but the same pace does not need to be maintained throughout. Varying the pace, and breaking up the lesson into shorter activities, will help all pupils and the better include those with any learning problems.

The planning for this type of lesson fits in well with the Key Stage 3 Strategy that recommends a three part lesson: a whole class session, group work, and then a plenary. Changing the seating arrangements, and giving students the chance to stand for a while or sit on the floor, will enhance learning and minimise disruptive behaviour. Where sitting behind a desk for the whole lesson cannot be avoided, give pupils the chance to stand up, move around, and stretch at least twice.

Practical experiences and apparatus

When planning to include pupils with learning difficulties, identify every possible opportunity for them to use practical, hands-on equipment and engage in firsthand experiences. Abstract concepts will not be understood unless linked to real-life, concrete examples and experiences. They might hear about wind power in science, but they need to feel the force of the wind for themselves to understand it. Let them fly a kite, hold a windsock, or just walk across the playground on a windy day.

If a maths class is working on fractions, give the pupil with learning difficulties a piece of card to cut into halves, quarters and eighths. Teachers sometimes find that the practical activities throw up challenging questions. In a lesson on 2D shape, a pupil would not accept the plastic shapes that were offered. She insisted the shapes were 3D because she could see the 1 millimetre edges. How thin does a 3D shape have to be to become 2D? Not the kind of philosophical question one would expect from a pupil with learning difficulties, but often they bring fresh perspectives that challenge assumptions.

Other sensory cues

One sense that people who have suffered brain trauma very much miss is the sense of smell. Not only is the sense of smell linked to taste, it also has powerful links to memory and emotions. Think of cordite in the air on Bonfire Night, the Christmas turkey roasting in the oven, the chemistry labs. Can you smell them right now?

It is possible in lessons to use the senses of smell and taste to increase concentration and aid memory. Try having indigenous plants and foods in the classroom when learning about a new country in geography, incense or myrrh in an RE session about Christian faiths, or a couple of fresh baguettes in the French lesson. A scented candle burning in the room will help pupils focus and remember the lesson when they are trying to recall facts for homework. Chapter 5 gives more detail about additional visual and sensory supports for learning.

Verbal delivery

Have you listened to yourself when you are teaching? Very few teachers have recorded their lessons and really listened from a pupil's perspective. It is a fascinating exercise and very worthwhile. Teachers are good communicators. They have a lot to say and they say it well. But they say it fast. Teachers also move around and do other things as they speak; they turn to face the whiteboard, give out books or write a note. A slower verbal delivery actually helps both the teacher and the pupils. It gives the teacher time to think and choose words more carefully. It means pupils understand more of what is being said. Look at the pupils when speaking to the class so they can see your face, and use eye contact and gesture to enhance the meaning of what you say.

One question at a time

Asking questions is a vital part of teaching. Teachers ask questions to check understanding and knowledge, to develop pupils' thinking and to make lessons more interactive. Teachers often ask a question and then immediately ask it again, rephrased to aid understanding, but some pupils will have formulated the answer and have their hand up even before the teacher has finished asking the initial question.

Pupils with learning difficulties need time to hear and process the question, search for the information they need for the answer, formulate a response, and then answer. This will take longer than you think. A slow count of ten is a useful length of time to allow for a considered response. If, while they are still thinking, the teacher rephrases the question and asks it again, the pupil will need to start the whole process again. In effect, they are being asked a new question before having had the chance to answer the previous one. This scenario makes pupils with learning difficulties confused and sometimes distressed, and can frequently lead to challenging behaviour. One way to avoid this situation is to prepare the questions in advance for the pupil with learning difficulties. The pupil could work on them at home, or in tutorial time, so that he or she will be prepared when the questions are asked in class. Alternatively, the pupil could work with the TA in the lesson to be ready to respond to a question in the plenary.

Use of language

Using simplified language does not mean that teachers need to 'talk down' to pupils with learning difficulties. Again, problems often arise because teachers are such good communicators with wide vocabularies. When a pupil with learning difficulties is in the class, try to say what you mean. English is ambiguous, full of inference, homonyms and synonyms. Be aware that a pupil is likely to misunderstand spoken information if they do not have additional cues, such as objects, pictures or signs.

CASE STUDY **Joe**

Joe is in Year 7. He has Down's Syndrome. In an October maths lesson Joe suddenly begins talking animatedly about ghosts and trick or treating. No matter how much his teacher asks him to be quiet he goes on talking about Hallowe'en. Eventually, he is sent out of the room. He is very distressed. At the end of the lesson the teacher asks Joe why he talked about Hallowe'en in the lesson. 'You asked me about it. You asked me about witches!' he replies. The teacher thinks back to the sentence she used before Joe had begun to speak. It was, 'Joe, *which* is the larger amount?'

Joe did not mean to behave badly. He thought he was answering his teacher's question. As it was the end of October it was not unreasonable for Joe to expect the teacher to talk about Hallowe'en, especially as he was going to a Hallowe'en party a few nights later.

Subject-specific vocabulary

Subject-specific vocabulary that has other meanings can cause comprehension problems. A way around this is to give pupils a dictionary (or glossary book) for each subject. The words they need to know can be written in the book with a simple explanation of the meaning in the context of that particular subject. For example, the word 'difference' may mean 'unlikeness' in common usage but, when asked to find the difference between two numbers, pupils need to know that in the context of a maths lesson it means subtraction of the smaller number from the larger. When asked to draw a table in maths, do not be surprised if what you get is what you sit at to eat your tea! In science, words such as 'conductor' and 'solution' need to have their meaning in the context explained carefully. This sort of work can be valuable preparation for starting new topics and can be planned by the teaching assistant and/or given for homework. It can be a huge boost to self-esteem if a pupil with learning difficulties can explain to the class at the beginning of a lesson the definition of a newly introduced word.

Choices

Everyone needs to be able to make sensible choices if they are to lead independent lives in adulthood. The reality for most pupils with learning difficulties is that just about everything they do is directed by adults. Sadly, it is not uncommon to see pupils in Year 8 or 9 having their books opened for them and being handed a pen by a teaching assistant. It is interesting to have a member of staff monitor a pupil with learning difficulties over one or two days, to log how many opportunities the pupil has to make choices. If children are deprived of choice they will give up trying to think for themselves, and become over-reliant on adults for all their needs. Build opportunities for choice into lessons, as basic as which pen to use, who to work with, where to sit, etc.

Individual subject targets

Short-term subject targets that are understood by and agreed with the pupil with learning difficulties will provide the means of measuring progress over time. The targets may be linked to the pupil's Individual Education Plan or may refer to skills and information specific to the subject. Make the targets visible by sticking them in the front of the exercise book or in the pupil's homework planner and refer to them at the start and end of every lesson. The target needs to be worded in such a way that, when it is achieved, the pupil is able to say, 'Yes, I can do that'. For example, a target such as 'Solly will know six French words about the family: maman, papa, soeur, frere, grandmere and grandpere' is easy to record and assess; Solly understands what he has to learn and knows when he has achieved his target.

Recording

Thankfully, the days are long past when pupils spent hours each day copying down writing from the blackboard, although most recording in schools is still in writing, as are most of the ways that pupils show attainment. Nowadays, there are numerous alternatives to written methods that make recording more accessible and often more fun. Pupils making a video or audio diary can show greater understanding than in a written essay. Drawings or photo-montages often reveal great insight. Software packages, such as Clicker 4, give on-screen word banks and pictures that make writing less slow and arduous. Giving all pupils alternatives to writing can produce startling results, often for pupils without learning difficulties.

Children with all kinds of learning difficulties will face problems with note taking or recording information in class. For many, the problem will be the spelling or the required speed of writing. In most English lessons it will be necessary to work on written tasks, but in other subjects it is important to reflect on the purpose and necessity for the writing. The usual reason for note taking is to enable pupils to access information from the lesson for homework and future examinations. As long as that information is available, the format is not important. A simple summary or aide-mémoire can be prepared by the TA for example, and clipped into the pupil's folder – with a sentence or two added by the pupil, possibly dictated to the TA where time is limited.

Pupils with more significant learning difficulties will need to be offered alternatives to writing in order to record information for later revision. By accepting a range of methods of recording, teachers will be liberating pupils with learning difficulties from the tyranny of the pen. Some pupils with learning difficulties may think of a wonderful sentence but will have forgotten it by the time they have finished writing the first word. That doesn't mean that teachers should give up on developing pupils' writing ability, but there is little point in them simply copying an adult's writing that they do not understand and cannot read back. Here are some ideas for alternative ways of recording.

Photographs

For pupils with learning difficulties a cheap digital camera will revolutionise recording. Photograph pupils as they take part in practical activities or allow them to sequence a series of photographs of, for example, a science experiment.

Computers

Laptop or desktop computers with symbol software or Clicker 4 (Crick Software) grids give pupils with learning difficulties an independent way of recording what they have learned. Clicker 4 grids for a wide range of subjects at Key Stage 3 are available on the internet at www.LearningGrids.com. Most of the grids have been designed by teachers who put them on the website for others to use.

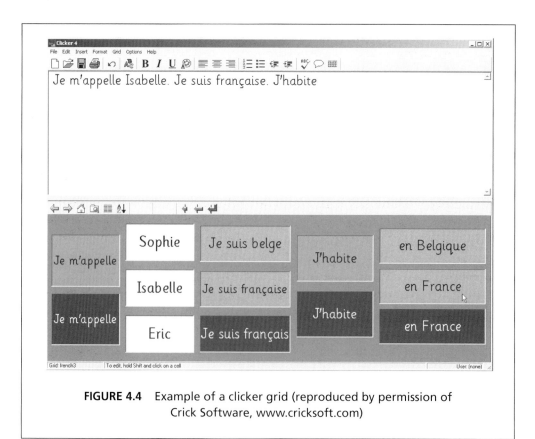

FIGURE 4.4 Example of a clicker grid (reproduced by permission of
Crick Software, www.cricksoft.com)

Drawings

Some pupils with learning difficulties are able to draw a picture based on what they have learned. They need to be able to look at the pictures at a future date and understand the meaning behind them. Asking the pupil to tell an adult about the picture, and scribing exactly what they say, will tell teachers how much the pupil has understood and learned.

Video and audio recordings

Recording lessons on audio tapes (or on video if you are feeling brave) gives pupils the option to listen to or watch the lesson again at home. Where the purpose of note taking and recording is to give pupils information to revise for future examinations, audio or video recordings will serve that same purpose in a more accessible format. Allowing pupils to record their own interpretation of the key lesson objectives, on audio or video tape, quickly builds up a bank of resources that can be used both for recording and for assessment. Teaching the pupil to speak each sentence into a Dictaphone, and then rewinding and listening as they write, frees them from the need for one-to-one support.

Sequencing

'Death by Worksheets' is a common feature of school for pupils in Key Stage 3. Worksheets are useful for differentiating work for different abilities in the class, and where the worksheets are well designed most pupils enjoy completing them. A useful way of developing skills for pupils with learning difficulties through worksheets is to design the worksheets as a cut and stick sequencing activity. Pictures and corresponding sentences can be mixed up on the worksheet. The pupil cuts them out and sequences the pictures in the right order and then matches the sentences. No matter what the subject, this approach works well. The pupil does not need to write, and the activity involves fine motor skills, reading and, if organised as a paired or group activity, speaking and listening.

Cloze procedure

Simple cloze procedure worksheets are useful for pupils who can read but who find writing and spelling difficult. These worksheets can easily be differentiated with the missing words and symbol supports at the bottom or at the side of the page.

Scribing

Scribing is a valuable technique to use when teachers really want a pupil's ideas and creativity to shine through. Pupils can either speak directly to another pupil or an adult, or they can use a tape recorder. Structuring the scribing with questions, pictures or objects will avoid the pupil losing the thread of what they want to say. In an English lesson on poetry, give a pupil with learning difficulties an object to hold – an orange perhaps. Let the pupil feel it and write down the words they use – smooth, round. Peel it – soft, furry. Smell it – fresh, fruity, tangy. Taste it – sharp, sweet, juicy. Put the words together and you have the basis of a poem.

Alternative ways of recording and presenting information

Photographs

On-screen word banks (Clicker 4, Writing with Symbols 2000)

Drawings

Audio tape

Video tape

Sequencing pictures and/or text

Cut-and-stick worksheets

Cloze procedure

Scribing

FIGURE 4.5 Alternatives to writing

Modern foreign languages

In many schools pupils with learning difficulties are disapplied from modern foreign languages, with the time so released often used for tutorials and extra work on basic literacy and numeracy skills. This is in many ways unfortunate, as learning a new language is the one area where pupils start from an equal basis. Pupils with learning difficulties do not bring to this new subject the memories of past failures and can be very motivated to learn. Teaching in modern foreign language lessons is also usually very lively and interactive, with many opportunities for active learning – and the promise of trips abroad in the future. Learning about different cultures and environments and even a few foreign words can enhance children's self-esteem and give them a real sense of 'belonging' within a mainstream peer group.

Assessment

Measure what you value rather than value what you can measure. Repeating this saying is not a mistake. For pupils with learning difficulties it is a necessity. For some pupils, one step up from P8 to Level 1 of the National Curriculum is as important an achievement as gaining five grade A to Cs at GCSE is for their peers. This book recommends setting a few precise targets in all subjects for pupils with learning difficulties. Precise targets are easier to assess and having only two or three targets limits the paperwork.

Where targets are based on P scales or National Curriculum level descriptors, pupils can be assessed against national benchmarks. This gives schools the information they need to show the value-added for a particular pupil. It is useful to have a system of observations of a pupil with learning difficulties across the curriculum which identifies successful strategies and gains impartial insights into pupil behaviour. The observations feed into the assessment process, and so into planning for future inclusion. A form for recording these observations can be found on the accompanying CD.

The most effective way of recording achievement for pupils with learning difficulties is by using progress files. A section for each subject can be filled with pieces of work, photographs and reports. A new file for each school year will build up a valuable record of the pupil's achievements and experiences over time.

Summary

The bases for successful inclusion in Key Stage 3 are:

- **Planning**: tracking back, key concepts, or curriculum overlapping, make it possible to plan to include a pupil with learning difficulties as part of the planning for the rest of the class.
- **Teamwork**: with other teachers, the SENCO, teaching assistants, and other professionals.
- **Flexibility**: accept different ways of recording and different ways of communicating.
- **Links**: make links between subjects explicit and visual.
- **Supports**: look beyond teaching assistants to peer support, visual and other sensory supports, and information technology.

Chapter 5 looks at support for inclusion in more detail.

Support for inclusion

☐ What is learning support?

The Index for Inclusion (Booth *et al.* 2000) defines learning support as 'all activities which increase the capacity of a school to respond to student diversity'. The authors of the Index clearly see learning support as a whole school issue, aimed at changing the school, rather than merely helping individual students. Learning support comes in many different forms, shapes and sizes, and to be most effective needs to permeate all areas of school life.

Support for learning will come from:

- teaching assistants and other adults;
- other pupils;
- visual and other sensory supports;
- information technology;
- outside agencies.

Support that is clearly defined, structured and consistent makes the difference between a successful long-term placement and one that ends in failure.

Among both teachers and support staff there are often fundamental misunderstandings about inclusion, and what inclusion really means.

People ask, 'How can it be inclusion if one pupil gets much more than another?'; or 'There are lots of pupils who would attain much more if they had a teaching assistant'; or 'It isn't fair that pupils with learning difficulties have teaching assistants while others don't'.

Everyone involved with pupils who have learning difficulties needs to be made familiar with the school's inclusive ethos and subscribe to its policy and practice. Appropriate training can help to shape attitudes and ensure that everyone is 'singing from the same hymn sheet'. The training activities below are a useful way of starting discussion and developing understanding about inclusion. They are suitable for use with school staff, governors, parents, and possibly older pupils.

| TRAINING ACTIVITY 1 | **Inclusion – definitions** |

Organisation: whole group together with one person scribing on flipchart.

Resources needed:
- paper and pens
- box
- flipchart

1. Each person writes a brief definition of inclusion.
2. The definitions are folded and placed in a box.
3. The box is shaken and everyone takes out a definition.
4. This definition is shared with one other person and key words noted, e.g. all, welcome, etc.
5. Write the key words on a flipchart.
6. As a group, use the key words to write a definition of inclusion that all can agree.

| TRAINING ACTIVITY 2 | **The 'No Buts' Zone** |

Organisation: all together, seated in a circle.

Resources: one red chair – the 'hot seat'.

The group moves around the circle, from one chair to the next. The person sitting in the 'hot seat' says something positive about including pupils who have learning difficulties, or they move on to the next chair without comment. A previously used comment may be repeated. The only rule is that no-one is allowed to say 'but'.

This is a very simple but powerful activity. Hearing the positive benefits of inclusion without the negatives – the 'buts' – can begin to change perceptions and attitudes.

| TRAINING ACTIVITY 3 | **On the cards** |

Organisation: groups of four people.

Resources:

- One envelope for each group.
- Each envelope to contain one card with the integration definition below, one card with the inclusion definition, and two blank cards.

| **Integration** A process by which individual children are supported in order that they can participate in the existing (and largely unchanged) programme of the school. | **Inclusion** A willingness to restructure the school's programme in response to the diversity of the pupils who attend. |

1. In the groups, open the envelope and set out the cards with the integration card on the left, the inclusion card on the right, and the two blank cards in between.
2. Discuss the definitions.
3. On the blank cards, write down two actions a school could take to move from the integration model to inclusion as defined on the cards.
4. As a plenary, write up all actions on a flipchart and discuss with the whole group.

Inclusion does not mean that everyone should receive the same provision, nor does it mean that all children should fit into the same systems in school. It is up to schools to adapt systems to meet the needs of a more diverse group of pupils and ensure that every pupil gets the provision that he or she needs. In *inclusive* schools everyone is entitled to the provision and support they need, and receives it regardless of ability.

All too often for pupils with learning difficulties in mainstream schools, the reality is that they spend every lesson sitting next to an adult and speaking only to adults. It is sad to see a pupil with learning difficulties working hard for every minute of the lesson with an adult making sure he or she stays on task. Look around the class, and you will see other students chatting quietly, gazing out of the window, or just day-dreaming. Very few pupils work consistently throughout lessons, yet often, this is what is expected of pupils with learning difficulties. They probably work harder than anyone else.

Teaching assistants and other adults

The growth in the number of teaching assistants in secondary schools has been a very positive development in recent years. The support given to groups or individual pupils by TAs can improve access to the curriculum, raise self-esteem, encourage positive behaviour and have a beneficial effect on the whole of the class.

It is important that teaching assistants are involved in subject planning so that they understand the purpose of the lessons, and can support pupils effectively. They should not be put in a situation of walking into a classroom to face a lesson about which they know nothing. Worse still are those occasions when a teaching assistant enters a classroom, and faces both a lesson and a pupil about whom they know nothing. It is a recipe for failure; and all too often it is the pupil who is blamed for 'spoiling the lesson' when becoming anxious and behaving in inappropriate ways.

No teaching assistant should be expected to work with a pupil, or group of pupils, about whom they have no knowledge or understanding. Equally, no pupil should be expected to work with an adult they do not know. Good working relationships between a pupil and a number of teaching assistants is the ideal situation in the secondary school. This can be achieved by scheduling several teaching assistants to support the pupil who has learning difficulties over the week. This variety of support also gives a variety of perspectives on the pupil's progress and attainment that informs assessment, target setting and reports.

Where teaching assistants are assigned to subject areas, their role should be to support the teacher in the delivery of the lesson. The higher level of subject knowledge gained by a teaching assistant working in subject areas creates an ideal situation – supporting teachers in the preparation of differentiated resources and activities, and in supporting pupils with learning difficulties.

However teaching assistants are managed, they should always be deployed in a way that fosters the independence of pupils, enabling them to be included in the class as fully as possible.

Support through transitions

In some instances, teaching assistants from primary schools move across with the pupil to the secondary school for the first few weeks of Year 7. This gives the pupil support through the transition from someone they know and trust and enables the teaching assistant to work alongside the secondary school staff, passing on knowledge and understanding. The short-term cost implications of this system need to be balanced by the savings likely to made from a pupil experiencing fewer difficulties in the longer term.

Transition to a new school is a major event for pupils, but moving up to a new year can also be traumatic. A new school year will involve a new timetable, new subjects, different rooms, new pupils and new adults, so an additional change of teaching assistant could lead to anxiety and inappropriate behaviour. Try to maintain the pupil's contact with at least one well-known teaching assistant during transitions from one school year to the next. Once the pupil is settled, staff can be changed without difficulties.

Individual support

The majority of pupils with severe learning difficulties have a number of support hours specified on their Statements of Special Educational Needs. These are often for all the hours they spend in the classroom. The close relationship that develops between a pupil with learning difficulties and the adult supporting them (sometimes for many hours each day) can be very positive. Equally it can become oppressive for both parties; in few other areas of life are two people forced to be together for up to seven hours a day, five days a week. Teaching assistants often cite a feeling of isolation when working with just one pupil, all day, every day, and there is often a high turnover of staff in one-to-one support work.

Where a pupil additionally has behavioural difficulties, the teaching assistant is often the only person who knows the pupil well enough to encourage him or her to stay on task; and too often the only person dealing directly with the inappropriate behaviours. This situation can cause intolerable stress and cannot be maintained in the long term.

Where a pupil has a large number of teaching assistant hours, it is always best to share those hours between at least two people so that if one is ill, another can provide cover. It also helps to prevent the pupil developing an over-dependency on one particular teaching assistant. They can also share ideas, strategies and tasks during 'overlap' periods when both are in school as well as giving one another moral support.

Support hours detailed on Statements need not tie a teaching assistant to a pupil for the amount of time specified. Schools are free to deploy teaching assistants to the best advantage of the pupils in the particular situation. Try adjusting working times for one or two days each week, so that teaching assistants arrive before the start of school, or stay after the end of the school day. These measures create opportunities to:

- talk to other teaching assistants;
- differentiate lessons with teachers;
- prepare resources;
- share training;
- attend staff meetings;
- contribute to annual review reports.

All these activities provide support just as much as having the teaching assistant sitting next to the pupil. Involving teaching assistants in planning, and giving positive feedback about their work, gives them the professional status they deserve.

Support for independence
- know when to stand back and encourage pupil to make own decisions
- expect pupil to work unsupported for part of each lesson
- develop independence in physical needs, such as using the toilet

Social interaction
- supporting pupil as member of a collaborative group
- promoting peer acceptance
- helping pupil develop social and organisational skills

Professional liaison
- working alongside teachers to plan curriculum access and set targets
- delivering programmes devised to meet specific needs
- observing and recording pupil responses
- monitoring behaviour, e.g. time spent on-task
- liaison with other professionals
- contributing to annual and transition reviews
- preparing appropriate resources

FIGURE 5.1 What support might look like

Support towards independence

All pupils need to develop individual and group working skills if they are to become independent adults. Standing back and allowing pupils to make their own decisions is a vital part of one-to-one support. Even when pupils need support for toileting or medication they should be encouraged to try to do as much as possible for themselves. It is very difficult to wean pupils off individual support once they become reliant on an adult, so they should work unsupported for part of every lesson, if at first for only five minutes. For this to be possible, teachers will need to give pupils activities that can be completed without constant support. Releasing the teaching assistant from supporting one pupil all the time also frees them to work with other students.

Social interaction

Wherever possible, pupils should work as part of a collaborative group, even if he or she has one-to-one support. Social interaction is enhanced when pupils work together, such as in a Jigsaw activity (see Chapter 3). Help with, and reminders about, personal organisation such as making a visual list of equipment needed for a particular lesson, or prompts such as 'What do you need for resistant materials tomorrow?', will develop confidence and independence. Other students are often unsure how to speak to and behave with a pupil with learning difficulties, and a teaching assistant can be a valuable role model for positive and equal interactions.

Professional liaison

Teaching assistants who support pupils on a one-to-one basis need to have time to talk to subject teachers, other than in lessons. This liaison must be timetabled and given a high priority by leadership teams if it is not to be eroded by other imperatives. By discussing the pupil together, the teachers and TA can ensure access for the individual pupil, and incorporate IEP objectives into lessons. Without this liaison, teaching assistants have to work in isolation, and may need to adapt inappropriate activities and resources while a lesson is taking place.

Teaching assistants often notice incidents in classrooms that teachers miss because of their necessary focus on the lesson, but they may have no time to pass this information on at the end of the period. A simple written format is a useful way of ensuring information is passed on and can be used as part of the assessment process and to inform planning of future lessons.

Comments written by teaching assistants should be predominantly positive. Try to start out by initially writing what the pupil has done well, and then comment on areas of difficulty. The following case study provides an example. A form that can be used by teaching assistants to record pupil responses is included on the accompanying CD.

CASE STUDY	Khalid

Extract from Khalid's Maths liaison form:

Year 7 Maths: Shape and Space: 3D shapes

Khalid sat quietly and listened to the first part of the lesson. He tried hard in the group activity and correctly named the cube and cuboid. Khalid had difficulty understanding the individual task. He became distressed and refused to attempt the work. When calm, he worked on a construction kit from his maths activity box. He created several 3D shapes. Digital photographs were taken of the finished shapes for Khalid's maths folder.

Written information about a lesson such as this gives a firm basis for assessing Khalid's level of understanding, and informs future lesson planning. It does not duck the issue of Khalid's inappropriate behaviour. It puts into context a task he did not understand, and shows how the difficulties were resolved.

Multi-disciplinary teams

Teaching assistants are a vital part of the multi-disciplinary team involved with a pupil, and close liaison with other professionals will be necessary, especially if the TA is to work with the pupil on, for example, a fine motor skills programme under the direction of an occupational therapist.

Other adults

Other adults in school – parents and grandparents, volunteers, student teachers, governors – are a great resource and an ideal way of helping pupils who have learning difficulties to develop social and interaction skills with a wider range of people. These people bring fresh perspectives and expectations, even new topics of conversation to expand a pupil's vocabulary.

Peer support

The most natural form of support for pupils who have learning difficulties comes from other pupils. Chapter 3 goes into detail about the various ways that peer support can be used. Peer support need not be a burden for anyone; rather, it can be a positive force for change in attitudes and behaviour right across the school.

Medication

The administration of medicines is an issue that causes schools much anxiety in planning to include pupils with learning difficulties. This medication could be regular, such as an inhaler for asthma, or medicine needed in an emergency situation such as after an epileptic seizure. Many pupils at some time need to take medicines in school, whether antibiotics for an infection or Ritalin to manage behaviour: training is needed to know how and when to administer various drugs – and good quality training *is* the key to raising staff confidence. To be sure that someone is available at all times, as many adults as possible need to be trained.

Other sensory supports

The day-to-day delivery of the secondary school curriculum relies on pupils being able to hear, understand, read and write at an appropriate level. Where pupils are unable to meet these criteria, other ways of delivering the curriculum need to be found, but experience has taught us that additional sensory supports will help all the class, not just those pupils with learning difficulties.

Visual supports

Visual supports include objects, photographs, drawings, symbols, signing, text, and moving images. Never underestimate the power of pictures or objects. Film is an important medium because it is so visual. Silent movies can deliver just as powerful a message as films with sound – sometimes even more so.

Visual languages such as symbols and signing support the development of reading and writing and aid communication.

Symbols
We are surrounded by symbols in everyday life – from road signs to the symbol above the fast food restaurant. Using symbols to support language and literacy builds on this natural pictorial communication. Symbols act as a bridge for pupils who have difficulties with literacy. It helps to sequence words and ideas, and frees intellectual development from the constraints of reading and writing. In text,

pictographic cues help pupils begin the decoding and encoding process. Symbols differ from text in that each concept is represented by one image rather than a group of phonemes. For example:

Dog

There are many words that have more than one meaning. By using symbols the intended meaning can be accurately represented. For example:

saw   saw   saw

Symbols:

- are internationally recognised;
- overcome language barriers;
- are pectoral or abstract;
- communicate ideas quickly and simply.

Symbolic development
While many symbols are iconic and easily recognisable, others are abstract. Pupils need to learn an abstract symbol in real contexts. As an instance, the symbol for 'dog' is a picture of a dog. Most children have experienced dogs in many different situations and their understanding of the concept 'dog' enables them to understand the symbol. The symbol for 'over', however, is abstract, and the pupil would need to learn the meaning of this symbol in real situations. The symbol for 'over' could be introduced when the child is climbing over a bench, or putting a cloth over a bowl. When introducing new concepts, always teach the pupil a symbol in context.

The understanding of symbols is hierarchical. Children need to understand a symbol in more than one manifestation before their understanding can be assumed. The progression for symbolic development is as follows:

- real objects
- representative objects
- photographs
- coloured pictures/drawings and line drawings
- standardised symbol systems
- written words (Kennard 1995a)

Real objects
Real objects exist in three dimensions. They can be touched, held and turned. They have form, size and textures. They can have taste and smell. Children at early stages of development need to have the symbol or sign introduced at the same time as they experience the object.

Objects are a powerful tool for supporting speech and text. Sensory boxes linked to Key Stage 3 texts bring the words to life. Pupils who find reading challenging can access the texts through audio tape, pictures, and objects together. They are thus enabled to give their interpretation of the text because they have had support for understanding.

Box 5.1	A sensory box for Macbeth

- a copy of the text
- a piece of tartan cloth
- a plastic cauldron containing toy mice, frog, insects, etc.
- a wooden spoon
- three witches' hats (from the local costume store)
- a cardboard crown
- a plastic knife
- a rubber glove dipped in red paint
- photographs of castles
- leafy branches
- tape of bagpipe music

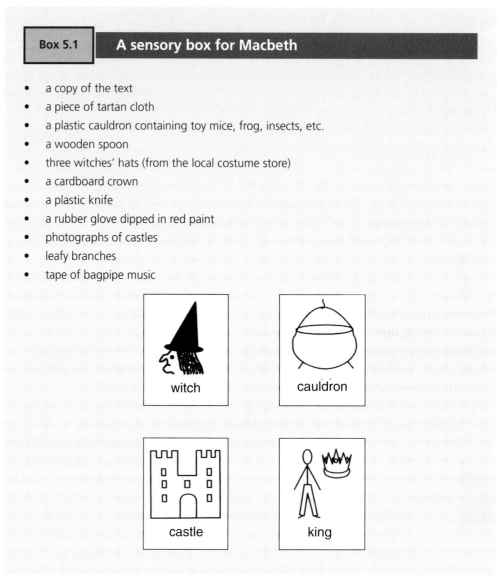

Representative objects

Representative objects are the next level of symbolic development. These are usually miniature objects, for instance a small plastic animal, or a toy vacuum cleaner. The pupil needs to understand that the small or toy object represents something real; for example, that a small plastic dog represents a real dog.

Photographs

Usually photographs are the first two dimensional representation presented to children. The change from 3D to 2D can pose real perceptual difficulties for some children, and at first photographs need to be presented in conjunction with either the real object or a representative object.

Photographs need to be used with caution because they can be very confusing. Pupils with learning difficulties are often given photographic timetables in school. Problems arise when photographs in the timetable are of the focus pupil working in different classrooms. One photograph looks very much like another. Where photographs contain too much visual information pupils will not be able to differentiate what is important and what is not. If photographs are used, they need to be of one object or one person on a plain background. Any more information will confuse pupils. For example:

> Julio has an autistic spectrum disorder. His visual timetable is made up of photographs, one of which is of the minibus that brings him to school. Every time Julio sees the photograph he says, 'Baa'. No-one can understand why he says this, nor will he say 'bus' or 'home' when he sees the photo. After several weeks, a teaching assistant notices a speck in the corner of the photo. Under a magnifying glass the speck is found to be a sheep in the distance. She cuts around the minibus in the photo and mounts it on card. Soon Julio is saying 'bus' when shown the picture of the minibus.

Coloured pictures/drawings and line drawings

If pupils are to use symbols and signs successfully, the ability to understand that a drawing represents a real object or situation is necessary. The drawings need to be clear and simple, with little or no background detail. If a pupil has experienced either a real dog or a toy dog, they will know that a dog has four legs, two ears, two eyes, and a tail. A drawing of a dog may show the dog sitting down or in profile. The pupil has to take his or her knowledge of a dog – four legs, two ears, etc. – and translate that knowledge into the two dimensional image of the picture below. This picture shows only two obvious legs, and neither a tail nor any ears or eyes. For adults this is obviously a dog, but this will be much less clear to pupils with learning difficulties. Such a picture would need to be introduced alongside representative objects or photographs.

Standardised symbol systems

Standardised symbols are the first clear link with reading. Just as a word has to represent a whole genus, so does a symbol. For example, a pupil may have a pet German Shepherd dog at home; a photograph can show an individual poodle; but the symbol has to represent all dogs, from Great Danes to a Jack Russell. Understanding this shift is an important developmental milestone.

There are a number of symbol systems that are used in schools. It does not matter which system is used, but it is important to decide on one, and stick to it to avoid confusion. Writing With Symbols 2000 software from Widgit has several symbol systems available that can be easily created by simply typing in the words. To support communication, the symbols can then be used in grids or to support text.

Written words

Understanding of the written word is the goal for all pupils. Symbols support reading development by giving visual cues above or below the words and can help to develop left to right tracking. Colour coding the symbols gives pupils an understanding of sentence structure.

Respiration symbols

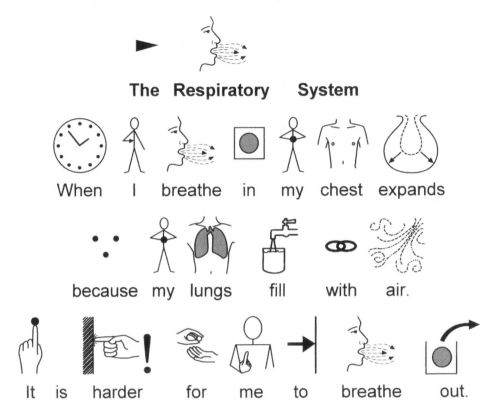

The following are some ideas on how to use symbols to support individuals and groups of pupils.

Visual timetables

Visual timetables (see Figure 5.2) are easy to make, and give vital support to pupils with learning difficulties. Symbols can be added to the usual school timetable or the symbols could be mounted onto card and fixed to a board with Velcro. This has the advantage of being easy to alter should any changes occur, such as for the Christmas concert or a visiting theatre group.

Communication boards

Communication boards are valuable tools in the classroom. They are unobtrusive but very effective. The boards are organised in a grid format that contains the pupil's most commonly used symbols. These can be general symbols such as 'toilet', 'drink', 'hurt', 'yes' and 'no', etc., as well as symbols for different subjects and/or photographs of key people. Bear in mind that it is important to teach symbols *before* they are added to a communication board. If the board is kept on the desk, the pupil, teacher or teaching assistant can point to the relevant symbol or photograph to support communication.

Communication books

A cheap A5 photograph album is ideal for this purpose. The pages hold a selection of small symbol cards, and a strip of Velcro on the front cover holds the pupil's chosen symbol sequence. The book also can be used by the adults working with the pupil to support understanding, and to let the pupil know what is to happen next.

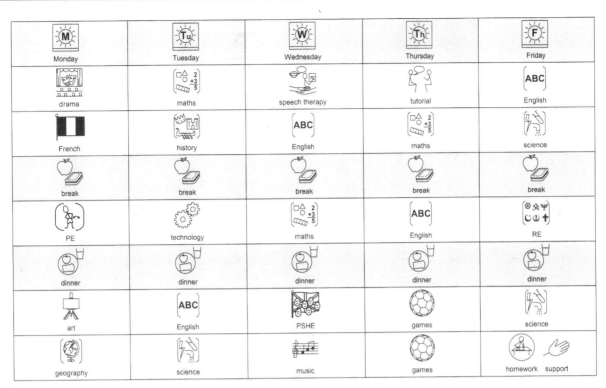

FIGURE 5.2 Symbols timetable

FIGURE 5.3 Communication board

PECS

The Picture Exchange Communication System (PECS) is a symbol system that was developed in the US and is available in the UK from Pyramid Education Consultants UK Ltd (www.pecs.org.uk). PECS is a structured programme that focuses on the initiation component of communication (Frost and Bondy 1998).

Access to information

As students move towards adulthood they need access to a wide range of important information that is usually text based; safety information, manuals for electrical equipment, recipes, menus, games instructions. All this vital information is easily translated into symbols using Writing With Symbols 2000 software. Information on sexual health, or the instructions on how to use a fire extinguisher, may even save a life. Symbol access to this information gives a measure of independence and develops self-advocacy, and enables people to make their own life choices.

Other symbol supports for communication

Some pupils are very reluctant to use large communication boards or books outside the classroom. Adolescent pupils do not want to appear different, and so need a more subtle approach. A small personal organiser will hold sufficient symbol cards to support communication between students in the canteen, or on the school bus. For students who need only a few symbols, laminate the cards and attach them to a key-ring. This will give easy access in less formal situations.

Memory mats

Memory mats are a valuable resource for pupils who need visual reminders to help them remember commonly used information. The mat is made of a piece of A3 card with space for a book marked out in the centre. Around the edge of the mat are written the letters of the alphabet, important subject-specific vocabulary, days of the week and months of the year, numbers and number words to 20 – any

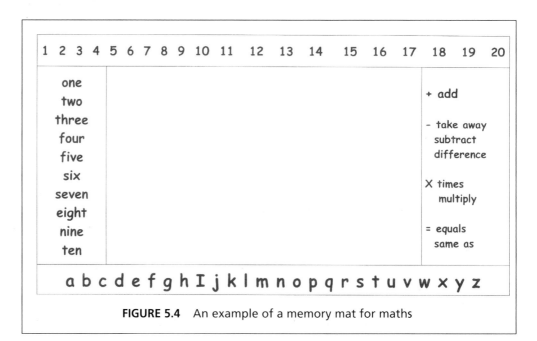

FIGURE 5.4 An example of a memory mat for maths

information that will support the pupil and aid independent working. The mats will last for a long time if they are laminated. The pupil may either have one mat that is kept in his or her bag, or a different mat can be created for each subject.

Signing

Just as symbols are all around us, so all of us use signing to some extent – but we call it gesture. We point, we touch, and we wave our arms around. Many people find it impossible to communicate without using their hands. Gesture is a means of adding nuance to speech, and it helps listeners to understand.

Less than ten per cent of our understanding of language comes from the words we hear. The remainder of our understanding comes from the context, facial expression, body language, tone of voice, and gesture. Children with learning difficulties often have difficulty understanding and using the full range of communicative skills. They may be able to use facial expression, but might not be able to understand the minute sophisticated changes between a smile and a sneer – a small facial movement that makes a huge difference to the meaning.

Signing supports communication both by giving pupils with learning difficulties a visual support for understanding speech, and by enabling them to make themselves better understood. Signing provides the means for them to let others know what they think about life in general, and school in particular. Impaired communication further excludes pupils with learning difficulties from other areas of school life, such as clubs and social events. Signing provides support to help pupils relax with each other, and share experiences. Teaching all the school to sign one or two songs for the Christmas carol service will boost both the self-esteem of pupils with learning difficulties and the signing skills of the whole community. As part of the concert, teach the congregation the signs for the chorus of one of the carols – it's quite a moving sight to see a large group of people signing together.

There are several signing systems in use in the United Kingdom. The most commonly used are Signalong and Makaton (Grove and Walker 1990). Both are based on British Sign Language (BSL), and are sign supporting systems that follow English word order. The primary purpose of these signing systems is to assist communication in cases of language difficulties associated with learning disabilities (Kennard 1992).

Parents are sometimes concerned that their child will stop trying to speak if they are taught to sign, but the opposite is the case. Signing both supports and encourages children to speak, and signs are only ever used in addition to speech. As with symbols, pupils gradually build up a vocabulary of signs, and start with commonly used words, such as mummy, good, hello, book, etc. Again as with symbols, signs must be taught with real objects or in real situations if pupils are to attach the correct meaning to the sign.

If signing is to be effective and useful, other people in school need to be able to sign at the same level as the pupil with learning difficulties. This will involve training for parents, teachers, teaching assistants, and other pupils. An ideal way of introducing signing is to teach the whole school community. Regular signing assemblies, and after-school or lunchtime signing clubs, are always popular. As the systems are based on BSL signing is a valuable and marketable skill in the workplace.

Schools that have developed the use of signing find there are benefits for a large number of pupils: those with minor hearing loss caused by colds or glue ear;

pupils with receptive language difficulties; and pupils with attention disorders. A visual component added to speech will not impede more able pupils, and will support many others. Signing has the extra benefit of slowing down speech – only a very skilled signer can sign at the usual rate at which people talk. Signing also encourages adults to use more simplified and direct language.

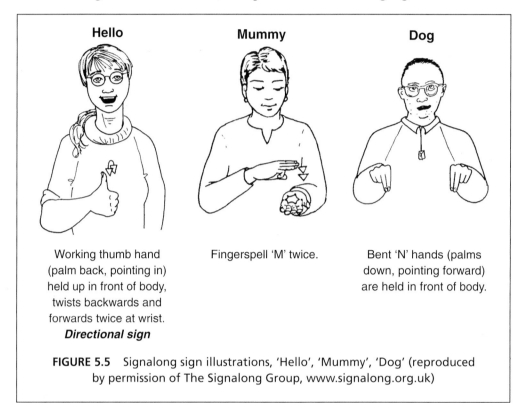

FIGURE 5.5 Signalong sign illustrations, 'Hello', 'Mummy', 'Dog' (reproduced by permission of The Signalong Group, www.signalong.org.uk)

The benefits of signing are, in short:

- supports receptive and expressive communication;
- is a valuable skill for all;
- slows down and simplifies speech;
- encourages independence and self-advocacy;
- enables communication between peers;
- increases participation in school life for pupils with learning difficulties.

Computers

Ten years ago the hope was that all children with communication or learning difficulties would have access to individual computers that would speak and write for them. That is taking rather longer than was originally thought, but the technology is now available to give appropriate technological support to facilitate pupils' communication and help them to access the curriculum.

Laptop computers

Laptop computers loaded with a talking word processor or Clicker 4 will increase independence for pupils with learning difficulties. Adding other software to meet individual needs will support learning across the curriculum. Software such as concept mapping, maths, and spelling programs will also help pupils develop basic skills. There are a number of low-cost computers available which are robust, and that are ideal for use in the classroom. Pupils learn how to use the machines quickly, and then are better able to take a full part in lessons. Self-esteem is also improved, especially for pupils in Years 10 and 11. All the information is easily transferred to printers or desktop computers.

Use caution when introducing computer-based learning to pupils with autistic spectrum disorders (ASD). Pupils with ASD can be reluctant to stop working on the computer, or will refuse to work on the programs decided by the teacher. This can become a trigger for challenging behaviour. A way to avoid this situation is to give the pupil a visual schedule for the lesson, and to put the computer work at the end. The schedule shows the pupil what he or she is expected to do before using the computer. This system also has the added benefit of motivating a pupil to finish the other work first. The bell at the end of the lesson will encourage the pupil to stop, and to move on to the next class.

CASE STUDY   **Jay**

Jay is in Year 8. He has a diagnosis of Asperger Syndrome. The school uses a computer-based learning system to support learning for pupils with special needs. Every time Jay uses the Successmaker program he becomes very excited and aggressive. He always looks forward to the computer sessions, but his teachers are reluctant to let him continue because he has damaged one of the machines.

Patrick, the school SENCO, offered to observe Jay in a computer session before the decision to withdraw him was finalised. Patrick noticed that Jay talked to himself whenever he worked on the computers, becoming increasingly angry. Jay repeatedly came out of the tasks to check his score. As he had only completed part of the task, his score was less than 100 per cent. Patrick quickly realised that Jay was misunderstanding the scoring system and this was the reason for his challenging behaviour. Jay knew he was answering all the questions correctly, but was still scoring less than 100 per cent.

Patrick recommended that Jay work on different programs with a non-accessible scoring system. Jay soon settled into the new programs, and there was no repetition of the challenging behaviour.

Switches

Switches are used with computers to replace a keyboard keystroke or mouse click. Switches can be used at a basic level to develop a pupil's understanding of cause and effect by changing images on a screen by pressing the switch. Using scanning, switches give pupils access to computer programs. Scanning is a switch technique in which a program highlights one at a time choices available for selection. By activating a switch the pupil makes a choice when the item they wish to choose is highlighted. The choices available may be just two items, or may be more complex choices that allow pupils to control all the functions of the computer. Switches enable pupils to operate electrical equipment for their own use, such as a fan or a CD player.

Some switches can be used as communication devices. 'Big Mack' switches record a message that can be replayed as many times as the pupil presses the switch.

Resources

Under Part 4 of the Disability Discrimination Act (1995), schools are not required to provide 'auxiliary aids and services'. Schools are not required to make physical alterations to buildings and the physical environment, for these are covered by the longer-term planning duties for LEAs and schools. Nor are schools required to provide auxiliary educational aids and services, the specialist equipment that is necessary to meet a child's identified needs. This would include, for example, a radio microphone for a pupil with a severe hearing impairment. Outside these exemptions however, there is a range of equipment that all secondary schools could reasonably be expected to have available. Much of this equipment is comparatively low cost, and useful to support a number of pupils with both temporary and permanent difficulties. Equipment such as:

Sloping writing surfaces
Adjustable height chairs
Triangular pen and pencil grips
Easy-grip scissors
Big Books for Key Stage 3 (available from the Key Stage 3 strategy and on www.standards.dfes.gov.uk/keystage3/publications)
Stress balls

Software
Writing With Symbols 2000 (Widgit Software)
Inclusive Writer (Inclusive Technology)
Clicker 4 (Crick Computing)
Kidspiration (Inclusive Technology)
Life Skills (Inclusive Technology)
WordShark (Inclusive Technology)
NumberShark (Inclusive Technology)
IEP Manager (SEMERC)

Access devices
Trackerball
Joystick
Switches
Big Mack communication device

Information and support on the above hardware and software is available from companies such as Inclusive Technology and Semerc, who have consultants who are also teachers. The consultants will visit schools and offer expert advice and training on your teaching and departmental needs.

Support toolboxes

Some schools provide their teaching assistants with support toolboxes. These small toolboxes can contain a variety of equipment that will support pupils in lessons. Much of the equipment in the toolbox is easily available in school, but it is more time efficient to have it all together and to hand. The toolbox could contain:

stapler	scissors	triangular grips	sticky labels
sticky tape	paper fasteners	rubbers	highlighter pens
pens and pencils	treasury tags	stress ball	calculator
small ruler	plastic wallets	Blu-tack	rubber bands
paper clips	coloured pens	Velcro	Dictaphone

Outside agencies

Professionals from other agencies are a fantastic source of information and of ideas for support for pupils with learning difficulties. Some agencies, such as occupational therapists, may work directly with parents. Parents will usually pass on booklets and/or therapy programmes that can be incorporated into staff training or the school timetable. Always try to find out what therapy targets a pupil is working towards, even if the therapy takes place in clinic or at home.

Invite to the annual review meeting all the professionals who work with a pupil. The prime purpose of the meeting is to review the pupil's Statement of Special Educational Needs, but the meeting is an ideal forum to share information and help professionals from outside education gain an understanding of how the pupil is being included.

Summary

When planning support for inclusion, see if you can find additional, more creative, ways of supporting pupils who have learning difficulties. Utilising other adults and peer support, as well as teaching assistants and teachers, is not only more effective in practice – it's more cost-effective too. The pupil who has learning difficulties benefits from being part of a wider social circle that demands and develops different social skills. Let's consign the 'velcro' teaching assistant to history!

Chapter 6 shows how the P scales can be used in secondary schools.

6 P scales and Individual Education Plans

Government initiatives drop through school postboxes with alarming regularity. Sometimes, these initiatives merely add to the bureaucratic burden; sometimes a real gem slips through almost unnoticed. The P scales are just such a gem. Designed originally to facilitate whole-school target setting for special schools, the P scales are a perfect assessment tool for tracking the attainment of individuals and of groups of pupils. In fact, they provide a common vocabulary for assessing pupils in all settings, but many mainstream secondary schools still do not realise what a powerful aid the P scales can be.

The P scales are important and powerful. Important because they are the first attempt to link directly to the National Curriculum levels the attainments of pupils with more significant learning difficulties; powerful, because they enable mainstream schools to meet the needs of pupils with learning difficulties. Along with the Guidelines for Planning, Teaching and Assessing the Curriculum for Pupils with Learning Difficulties (QCA 2001a), the P scales give schools excellent advice and support on including pupils working below Level 1 of the National Curriculum.

What does the P stand for?

The P scales are designed to measure the attainment of pupils working below Level 1 of the National Curriculum. The original P (performance criteria) scales document was published by the Qualifications and Curriculum Authority (QCA) in 1998 (revised in 2001) and was designed to support the target setting process for individuals and schools in English, maths and science. The Guidelines for Planning, Teaching and Assessing the Curriculum for Pupils with Learning Difficulties were published three years later and include P scales, from P1 to P8, in all National Curriculum subjects and Personal, Social and Health Education and Citizenship. They are a valuable resource for all schools and particularly useful where schools need to demonstrate value-added attainment for pupils with learning difficulties. Knowledge and understanding of the P scales could be a part of schools' anticipatory response to Part 4 of the Disability Discrimination Act (1995) as set out in the Disability Rights Commission Code of Practice for Schools (Disability Rights Commission 2002).

The P scales provide eight descriptions that lead up to Level 1 of the National Curriculum, termed P1 to P8. The performance descriptions for P1 to P3 are common across all subjects, and are designed for pupils with profound and multiple learning difficulties who need to access the curriculum through sensory activities and experiences. There are two differentiated descriptions within each of levels P1 to P3, termed (i) and (ii) within each level.

For example, in science:

P2 (i) Pupils begin to respond consistently to familiar people, events, and objects. They react to new activities and experiences (i.e. discarding objects with unfamiliar textures). They begin to show interest in people, events, and objects, *for example, leaning forward to follow the scent of a crushed herb.* They accept and engage in coactive exploration with the help of another, *for example, feeling materials in hand-over-hand partnerships with a member of staff.*

P2 (ii) Pupils begin to be proactive in their interactions. They communicate consistent preferences and affective responses, *for example, showing a consistent dislike for certain flavours or textures.* They recognise familiar people, events and objects, (for example, moving towards particular features of familiar environments). They perform actions, often by trial and error, and they remember learned responses over short periods of time, *for example, rejecting food items after recent experience of bitter flavours.* They cooperate with shared exploration and supported participation, *for example, examining materials handed to them.* (QCA 2001b)

The text in italics shows subject-specific examples.

The P scales in English and maths each have three differentiated descriptions within Level 1 and Level 2 of the National Curriculum. The elements in English are: speaking and listening, reading and writing. In maths the elements are: using and applying mathematics, number, and space, shape and measures.

The English and maths criteria are consistent with the Primary Literacy and Numeracy Strategies enabling teachers to track back from the Key Stage 3 frameworks for English and maths, through the primary frameworks, and into the P scales. It is then possible to identify objectives appropriate to a pupil's ability that can be addressed in age-appropriate contexts. P8 reflects the performance described in the Early Learning Goals and Reception objectives in the Early Years Framework for Teaching.

How can the P scales be used in secondary schools?

The P scales give secondary schools the tools needed to set appropriate and achievable targets for pupils with learning difficulties and record small measures of progress. They provide a framework of common performance measures for benchmark information, and for the calculation of value-added improvement for pupils working at these levels (QCA 2001b). They support the detailed assessment of pupil attainment for reports and records of achievement and offer ready-made objectives for Individual Education Plans.

When used alongside the Key Stage 3 strategy, P scales give teachers a means of differentiating work for classes that include pupils with a wide range of ability. They provide objectives appropriate to the abilities of a pupil with learning difficulties which can then be taught in age-related contexts with age-appropriate resources.

Where schools have a cohort of pupils working below or within Levels 1 and 2 of the National Curriculum, the P scales can be used as part of the whole-school target setting process. Where schools do not have sufficient numbers of pupils working below Level 1, they may create a cohort from pupils with learning difficulties from other local schools. This has an added bonus of allowing staff to compare pupils' progress, and to share ideas and resources.

The P scales across the curriculum

The curriculum guidance documents, Planning, Teaching and Assessing the Curriculum for Pupils with Learning Difficulties (QCA 2001a) include P scales, P1 to P8, for all National Curriculum subjects, PSHE and Citizenship.

These documents are meant as guidance only, but provide a sound foundation for planning, target setting and assessment. They give ideas for ensuring progression and age-appropriate experiences. In addition, they give advice and offer strategies for teaching pupils with a diverse range of needs.

Assessment

The P scales are an ideal assessment tool to use with pupils who have learning difficulties. They provide small steps towards, and within, Level 1 of the National Curriculum, which can be used as either subject or IEP targets. Several publications are available that break down the P scales into even smaller steps suitable for pupils with more significant learning difficulties. Some of these commercial publications include grids, for recording attainment and progression over time. These grids can be useful as evidence of attainment and progression, but it must be remembered that the P scales do not in themselves constitute a curriculum. It is not enough for pupils simply to work through the P scale objectives, either on their own or in a small group.

P scale objectives need to be taught in the context of subject lessons, with age-appropriate experiences and resources.

The P scales and English

The P scales for English are divided into three components:

- speaking and listening
- reading
- and writing.

These components tally with the strands in the National Literacy Strategy for primary schools, and the English framework for the Key Stage 3 Strategy. The National Literacy Strategy (NLS) has produced a Strand Tracker document for non-fiction objectives (NLS 2002) (available on-line at www.standards.dfes. gov.uk/literacy/publications) that shows individual strands of the literacy framework from Year 6 to reception. Strand trackers are particularly useful when tracking back to objectives appropriate for pupils with learning difficulties to link with later stages. This enables teachers in secondary schools to track back through the Key Stage 3 Framework, the Primary Literacy Strategy framework and into the appropriate P scale matching the pupil's level of attainment. In secondary schools, when teaching English to pupils with learning difficulties it is necessary to ensure progression in terms of context and materials, as well as skills. Pupils can access some elements of most texts, or related or adapted texts could be used. Several publications now offer adapted texts based on Key Stage 2 and Key Stage 3 books. These publications include passages of simplified and symbol supported text (see Figure 6.1). They also include lists of sensory resources that can be used to support access to the texts for pupils with profound and multiple learning difficulties.

The P scales and maths

The P scales for mathematics also are divided into three components:

- using and applying mathematics;
- number;
- and shape, space and measures.

Excellent materials have been produced by the Key Stage 3 strategy, based on the primary maths framework and the P scales. Especially useful is the Accessing the National Curriculum for Mathematics (DfES 2002) document that gives examples of what pupils with SEN should be able to do at each P level. It is designed to be used alongside the Framework for Teaching for Years 7, 8, and 9. These materials make tracking back relatively quick and simple and can be obtained from Key Stage 3 maths consultants or on the DfES website at www.dfes.gov.uk/keystage3/strands/publications. Offering pupils a wide range of active and relevant maths experiences will be important in maintaining motivation and attention. Applying mathematical concepts in real-life contexts will help pupils to generalise skills and consolidate their understanding.

Text for pupils working at levels P5–6

Stop! Stop the storm,

says Miranda.

FIGURE 6.1 Example of symbol-supported text from *The Tempest* (Walker, Davis and Berger 2002)

The power of positive target setting

Setting targets for pupils with learning difficulties is the only way to ensure their particular learning needs are being met. Positive targets achievable within a realistic timescale drive forward both progress and attainment. The pupil knows what he or she is expected to learn, and by when. The teacher and teaching assistant can measure progress easily, and adjust targets, teaching methods and support to match the pupil's changing learning needs. If merely *present* in lessons that are not differentiated, and for which the pupil has no individual objectives, he or she will learn very little. With positive targets that are addressed in the lessons through differentiated activities and resources, and based on the key concepts method or curriculum overlapping (see Chapter 4), the teacher can be confident that the needs of the pupil with learning difficulties are addressed.

The power of positive target setting lies in a pupil's sense of achievement and success. For a pupil who may never have known the feeling of pride in their work, realistic targets will guarantee success. Celebrating that success each time the pupil achieves their target will build the motivation to try harder the next time. Targets may not be the same as those for everyone else, but they are no less important or effective for that. Socially and educationally, the 'cycle of success' can transform a pupil.

Small steps to success

Attainments made by pupils with learning difficulties are no less valid than those of pupils working towards GCSE or AS or A level examinations. The progress made may be in small steps, but that progress is gained through enormous effort and determination. What is meant here by success? For pupils with learning difficulties, success can mean making progress against realistic IEP and subject targets. It can mean being independent in class. It can mean making friends and maintaining relationships. The P scales can support this success when used as a scaffold to help both the school and the pupil move forward and upward. With the P scales, teachers can identify the next small step, and they can look back at the end of a school year and see just how far the pupil has travelled. Delight when a pupil achieves P8 and moves into Level 1 of the National Curriculum is no less real for a pupil in Year 9 than for a child in Year 2.

More than 'working towards'

Until the advent of the P scales, pupils with learning difficulties were often assessed at W – working towards Level 1 – for their entire school careers. No matter how much real progress pupils made, that progress could not be reflected in terms of National Curriculum attainment. Parents would become demoralised to see 'W' on annual reports year after year, causing them sometimes to question whether their child had made any worthwhile progress at all.

When, in 1998, the first P scales document was published, this was all changed. At last teachers could show progression leading into the National Curriculum, and parents could see their children on the same track as others. The P scales gave a common framework and language for assessment for all pupils. At last special schools could at last measure what they valued, and celebrate just how much progress could be made by their pupils.

IEP targets

The P scales for English and maths can be used very effectively as the basis of targets for Individual Education Plans. Each of the level descriptions contains a number of sentences that may either be used individually, or joined together to create an IEP target. For example:

> Cristina in Year 7 is working at P7 in English and maths. Cristina has a speech and language disorder, and a general developmental delay.

English: Writing:

> P7: Pupils group letters and leave spaces between them as though they are writing separate words. Some letters are correctly formed. They are aware of the sequence of letters, symbols and words. (QCA 2001b, p. 25)

An IEP target based on this P scale for Cristina in Year 7 could be:

> Cristina will spell her first and last names correctly.

Maths: Number:

> P7: Pupils join in rote counting to ten. They count at least five objects reliably. They begin to recognise numerals from 1 to 5 and to understand that each represents a constant number or amount. They respond appropriately until to key vocabulary and questions. Pupils begin to recognise differences in quantity. In practical situations they respond to 'add one' and 'take one'. (QCA 2001b)

An IEP target based on this P scale for Cristina in Year 7 could be:

> Cristina will recognise numerals 1 to 5 and link numerals to sets of objects.

The P scales for Personal, Social and Health Education and Citizenship can be used to inform IEP targets for PSHE. This linkage will give teachers an understanding of the comparative level of a pupil's social functioning.

Using the P scales to plan for progression

Progress is not always linear – onwards, upwards, better! For pupils with learning difficulties we may have to re-examine just what we mean by progress. Progress can mean learning new skills, but it could also mean practising, maintaining and extending existing skills. Pupils with learning difficulties continue to learn and make progress throughout their lives. The myth that pupils with learning difficulties reach a 'plateau' in their learning, and subsequently learn nothing more, is just that – a myth. As with all children, pupils facing additional challenges such as family breakdown, illness, or even the worst ravages of puberty, will have a slower rate of progress. When pupils are making significant progress in one area, sometimes the rate of development of other skills may slow down.

No matter how wonderful our teaching may be, or how many targets we set, there will be a progressively widening gap between the attainment of pupils with significant learning difficulties and other pupils. The answer to this is not to propose that the pupil should go somewhere else because they cannot cope with a mainstream curriculum. There should not be an assumption that pupils will all progress at the same rate. The answer is to accept the widening gap – often easier for teachers than for parents – and then to discount it. It is unnecessary and unfair continually to compare pupils' levels of ability. What matters is that pupils make adequate progress against the targets set for them as individuals in IEPs and in the curriculum subjects.

The general guidelines (QCA 2001a) recommend that planning for progression for individuals or groups might focus on the following.

Developing skills

As well as learning new skills, pupils with learning difficulties will benefit from opportunities to revisit skills learned previously, to generalise learned skills into different contexts, and to practise and maintain skills. For example, pupils will learn to measure using standardised units in maths. This skill can be practised regularly in textiles, food technology, and art and design.

Curricular content

As pupils grow and move through the Key Stages it is necessary to ensure they have access to new knowledge and experiences. The breadth of the learning experiences should not be limited because of their learning difficulties. A broadening curriculum throughout Key Stages 3 and 4 will extend pupils' knowledge and understanding. A developing awareness of personal, health, ethical and environmental issues will help pupils begin to make informed decisions about their own lives. For instance, an understanding of what constitutes a healthy diet may help a pupil make changes in his or her eating patterns, and so avoid potential health problems in later life.

Contexts for learning

Teachers may support progression by planning opportunities for pupils to apply skills, knowledge and understanding in new contexts. Give pupils access to a variety of experiences, activities and environments appropriate to their chronological ages, interests and prior achievement. This will help them generalise skills and understanding. While in Key Stage 3 a pupil can expect to work in classrooms but will also need to learn in school workshops, studios and laboratories. In Key Stage 4 it would be appropriate for pupils to extend their learning into community and workplace settings, such as a local college of technology, or community theatre. Tracking back to find appropriate objectives from earlier key stages should always then be linked to age-appropriate contexts. For example, a pupil in Year 8, working on objectives from YR of the numeracy strategy in maths, would not learn how to use a calculator *unless* the YR objectives were taught in the context of the Year 8 lesson. This is because calculators are not included in the framework for Year R.

Resources

Offering pupils a differing range of resources over their time in a school is an important part of progression. Pupils with learning difficulties can become bored if they are expected always to work with books and equipment from Key Stage 1. It can be useful to borrow resources from a local primary school, to give teachers ideas for differentiation in the secondary school. It is not appropriate, however, simply to import infant workbooks for secondary pupils to use. In Year 7 it would be appropriate for a pupil with learning difficulties to use counters or Multilink cubes to support counting activities. In Year 11, the same pupil may still need to develop counting skills, but development would need to be addressed through work-based, real-life activities, such as making up sets of components or preparing ingredients for cooking as part of an accredited course.

Teaching methods and support

As the pupil with learning difficulties moves through the school, progression may be shown in the form of differing methods of teaching and support. These differences will be determined by pupils' individual strengths and learning styles. A move away from more formal teaching methods allows pupils to negotiate their learning needs with their teachers. This can be challenging for pupils with learning difficulties and for teachers too, as it involves both sides taking risks. Pupils need to learn how to improve their own learning and performance; gradually they can take more responsibility for setting their own learning goals, and for keeping their own records of achievements. This progression towards independent thinking and learning is particularly important in Key Stage 4.

To show progression, the style and level of support received by a pupil could be changed. Gradual reduction in the level of adult support, and a greater expectation of cooperation between students, would support progression towards independence.

Problem solving

Everyone needs to develop problem solving skills, but pupils with learning difficulties have very few opportunities to solve problems either individually or in groups. Pupils can become over-reliant on adult support and reluctant to try new things, or it is sometimes considered that they are not able to contribute to group activities involving problem solving. This comes back to the need to allow pupils to take risks, to let them try things out, and sometimes to make mistakes. To develop the skills of problem solving, start with individual or paired tasks based on real, everyday activities. A visual or object framework in which to operate will give the pupil the support they need. For example:

Box 6.1	The Christmas party

A Year 8 form is planning a Christmas party. Each member of the form has a job to do to prepare for the big event. Charlotte is assigned the job of making sure there are enough party poppers. She is given a large bag of party poppers and a piece of card showing small photographs of all the pupils in the form. Her form tutor tells her that everyone has to have just one party popper. Charlotte cannot count the number of pupils – and there are a lot of poppers in the bag – and she 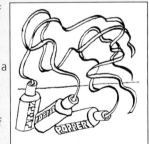 begins to look anxious. Another pupil comes over and puts one popper on one of the photographs. Charlotte then continues to put one popper on each photograph until they are all covered, leaving the remainder in the bag. Her form teacher complains that she hasn't put one out for him – but she tells him he is too old.

Photocopying the photographs made all the difference for Charlotte and she was able to play her part in the preparations for the party. Without the photographs she would have had to have one-to-one support to complete the task.

Setting small problems within other activities, where the pupil has to work something out to be able to continue, will help to begin the problem solving process. For example, in a science lesson on electricity the resources box contains everything the pupil needs to make a circuit, except a battery. The pupil has a diagram that shows the battery. She looks in the neighbouring box and checks the contents. Realising what is missing, she asks the teacher for a battery.

This small problem gave the pupil reasons to think, check, investigate, interact, and communicate. Involving pupils who have learning difficulties in group problem solving activities will further develop these skills. In group activities, such as treasure hunts around the school using picture and written clues, other pupils will model thinking and problem solving skills. Seeing and hearing how other people work things out is also an important part of the learning process.

Progression for pupils with profound and multiple learning difficulties

Pupils with profound and multiple learning difficulties (PMLD) may need to work at the same level of the P scales for one or more years. Their progression needs to be planned in terms of experiences, resources and contexts. Many pupils with PMLD access the curriculum through their senses, so need activities that involve active exploration: feeling different textures; experiencing different kinds of movement; tasting a range of foods; smelling perfumes, herbs and flowers; listening to music and environmental sounds; looking at, and through, colours and visual effects. Linking these sensory activities to age-appropriate subject contexts will ensure progression. Trying to give these experiences in isolation will create a stagnant situation that is not stimulating, either for the pupil, or for those adults working with the pupil.

CASE STUDY | **Jemma**

Jemma is in Year 10. She joins the GCSE art class for one lesson each week. She has cerebral palsy with profound and multiple learning difficulties. She uses a wheelchair for mobility in school, and spends part of each day in a standing frame. The Year 10 group is working on the relationship between three-dimensional design and urban, rural and other settings. Jemma's teacher, teaching assistant, and the other students, collected a variety of found materials from both the urban and rural environments. Together with the other students, Jemma explored these materials in conjunction with other sensory input. When creating structures using the urban materials, the students created harsh lighting and listened to garage music. The air was full of the odours of welding and melting plastic. They were surrounded by the sounds of metal being beaten and bent. Jemma found the lessons totally stimulating, looking around constantly, and vocalising to show her pleasure. Far from distracting the other students, the environment that was planned for Jemma helped all the students in the group to create more imaginative structures.

Jemma could have accessed these experiences in a specialist sensory room, full of bubble tubes, water beds and other expensive equipment. It would have been an excellent experience for her and she would have enjoyed it immensely. It would have been a different experience, but it would not have been better.

In the context of the GCSE art and design lessons, not only did she have access to age-appropriate materials and experiences, she was also among other young people of her own age who greeted her each week, chatted to her as she worked and kept her interested. Jemma enjoyed the sensory experiences, but it was the other students who really fascinated her. It was them that she loved to watch and to listen to.

P1 to P3

The earliest levels of the P scales, particularly P1 to P3, support schools in developing the curriculum to meet the needs of pupils with profound and multiple learning differences. The curriculum will need to give these pupils opportunities to develop their skills in:

- communication;
- interaction;
- understanding cause and effect;
- sensory awareness and perception;
- linking of objects, events, and experiences;
- predicting and anticipating.

With a little thought and creativity, these activities can be built into mainstream secondary lessons. Below is an example of a pupil with profound and multiple learning difficulties included in a Year 11 music lesson.

CASE STUDY | Ryan – Year 11 Music

AQA GCSE Music: Area of Study: Music for Special Events (50-minute lesson)

Ryan uses a wheelchair for all his time in school. He has always attended mainstream schools and loves the company of the boys in his year group. Ryan communicates by eye pointing and smiling.

Ryan is working at level P2(ii) of the P scales in music.

> P2(ii): Pupils begin to be proactive in their interactions. They communicate consistent preferences and affective responses. They recognise familiar people, events and objects. They perform actions, often by trial and improvement, and they remember learned responses over short periods of time. They cooperate with shared exploration and supported participation.

Ryan's objectives for the lesson at P2(ii)
To link music/sounds with events, objects and experiences (music).
To communicate consistent preferences by eye pointing (curriculum overlap).

Background
Ryan accesses the curriculum through all his senses. While listening is the primary sense used here, the team have collected resources that Ryan can touch, smell, taste and see, to heighten his understanding of the music. Three corners of the music room have been decorated to represent specific special events:

- Christmas

A small decorated tree, plastic baubles, paper chains, brightly wrapped parcels, a toy dancing Father Christmas, plastic holly, mincemeat, fruit cake, fake snow, mulled fruit drink, etc. A CD contains recordings of carols, feet scrunching in snow, the ringing of bells, etc. and music composed especially by the other students.

- A beach holiday

A bowl of sand, a bowl of water, a pair of flip flops, a sun hat, sunglasses, sun cream, orange squash, a lamp, towel, deck chair, a fan heater. A CD containing recordings of Viva España!, Summer Holiday, Agadoo, etc., the sea breaking onto the shore, and similar sounds, and music composed especially by other students.

- A wedding

A wedding dress, a smart suit, confetti, fizzy fruit juice, invitation, fruit cake, perfume, large hat/top hat, plastic flowers. A CD containing recordings of the bridal march, Here Comes the Bride, Vidor's Toccata, and hymns performed by students from the school.

Ryan spent several short sessions exploring each of the areas and getting used to the headphones before the unit of work started.

Each corner contains objects related to the occasion, and CDs prepared by the teacher and the other students in the group. Ryan has a personal CD player that he uses in the corner as, with his teaching assistant, he accesses the objects and experiences.

Activities

This is the fourth lesson of the unit. Ryan joins the group at the start of the lesson. The teacher greets the pupils, and gives a brief introduction and instructions for the lesson. The students are to work individually or in pairs on their compositions at the keyboards. (10 minutes)

Ryan's wheelchair is placed in the centre of the room where he can see the three prepared corners. He is asked to choose by looking at the corner in which he would like to work. Ryan then looks at all three corners of the room in turn, before holding his gaze on the beach holiday corner. (5 minutes)

His teaching assistant then wheels Ryan to the holiday corner, puts the CD in the personal stereo, and the headphones on Ryan's head. As he listens, the lamp and fan heater are turned on, and the sunglasses put on his face. Ryan smiles broadly at this but backs away when the hat is brought towards him, so this is left on the table. The teaching assistant puts the bowl of sand onto the tray of the wheelchair, and water is gently poured over Ryan's hands. He is asked if he would like to have his shoes and socks removed, to feel the sand and water with his toes, but again he draws back at this and so it is decided to ask again on a later occasion. Ryan is given a drink of orange squash. Sun cream is gently massaged into his arm (the sun cream was sent in by Ryan's mother to avoid any allergic reaction). (25 minutes)

The final ten minutes of the lesson are spent listening to each of the other students' compositions. Ryan is happy to listen as the students play, and his responses to the music are noted by his teaching assistant. Photographs and video recordings are taken at regular intervals as a record of Ryan's experiences, and as evidence of attainment against the P scales.

Physical, orientation and mobility skills

Pupils with profound and multiple learning difficulties will have additional priorities that will have to be addressed in school, of physical, orientation and mobility skills. These skills include:

- fine motor skills, such as grasping, holding, and manipulating;
- whole body skills, such as the coordination of movement, rolling, and walking;
- positioning skills, such as head control;
- tolerating and/or managing mobility aids, such as a wheelchair, walking frame, or splints.

These priorities usually can be addressed in mainstream classes, without recourse to specialist equipment.

Fine motor skills can be developed in:

- Art – working with a range of media and textures
- Technology – joining components
- Music – exploring and playing percussion instruments
- Maths – creating different sizes of sets of objects.

Whole body skills can be developed in:

- Drama – drama games
- Physical education – lying and sitting on the trampoline, gymnastics
- Dance – exploring body shapes, moving in time to music.

Positioning skills, and tolerating and managing mobility aids, will be developed in all lessons and other school situations. Practising these priorities in the supported setting of a school will prepare students for living and working in the local community and wider society.

Pupils with additional medical priorities

A concept of progress may be more difficult to define for those pupils who have significant medical needs in addition to profound and multiple learning difficulties. For pupils with degenerative diseases, progress may need to be defined in terms of maintaining, rather than extending, skills and understanding. Progress and progression can be defined in terms of the breadth of the experiences in which the pupil is involved. In this situation the P scales offer an objective benchmark for assessment, and strategies for developing appropriate provision, such as the use of communication aids, or ICT support for an individual pupil.

Individual Education Plans

What should an IEP look like?

No-one has yet has produced an Individual Education Plan (IEP) format which is perfect for all situations. IEPs can be A5, A4, A3 or foolscap size. They can be landscape or portrait. They can be handwritten, typed, or word processed. What matters is that the format works in your school for your pupils and is used consistently. When your school has decided on a format, then it is vital that all members of staff use the format agreed. The importance of this consistency should be made very clear to new members of staff who may bring with them a format used in their previous school. Inspectors and parents alike need to see IEPs that use a common format, that are clear, and that have direct relevance to the pupil's school experiences. It is a waste of time and effort to have IEPs that sit in a folder until they are brought out for review at the end of the term.

Individual Education Plans are working documents that constantly need to be at hand. Copies of IEPs should be distributed to each and every member of staff working with the student. For IEPs to be really effective, teachers and teaching assistants should be expected to scribble notes on them, to add post-its, even cut and paste some sections. If looking pristine when the time comes for review, then the IEP has been a waste of time. All copies of the IEP should be collected in and the notes and jottings collated to give a more rounded review than could be achieved solely by the SENCO.

The sheer number of IEPs used in some secondary schools is itself a barrier to effective provision for pupils with special educational needs. The burden of work is often unmanageable for a SENCO who is expected to write, monitor and review IEP targets at least once a term, in addition to other teaching and pastoral duties. The advent of computer software, such as IEP Manager (SEMERC), has undoubtedly helped to speed up the process, but the statements in these programs are often not sufficiently precise for pupils with more complex learning difficulties. Limit the number of targets to just three or four, as recommended by the SEN Code of Practice (DfES 2001), and this simplifies the process. Involve other teachers, teaching assistants and parents in the monitoring and review of the IEPs. This will share the work and support the professional development of colleagues.

The Special Educational Needs Code of Practice gives clear guidance on the precise information an IEP should include:

- short-term targets set by or for the pupil
- the teaching strategies to be used
- the provision to be put into place
- when the plan is to be reviewed
- success and/or exit criteria
- outcomes (to be recorded when the IEP is reviewed). (DfES 2001, p. 59)

The Code of Practice is very clear that an IEP should contain only targets that are additional to, or different from, the usual differentiated curriculum provision and expects all teachers to differentiate work, even where pupils are grouped in sets.

A good IEP will focus on three or four targets, and will relate to key areas in communication, literacy, mathematics, physical skills, and aspects of behaviour and social skills.

Additional priorities

An IEP will need to address additional priorities for some pupils at certain times. These priorities may include organisation and study skills, such as:

- attending and directing attention
- sustaining interest and motivation
- selecting and organising their own environment
- managing their own time
- completing a task
- taking responsibility for tasks.

For certain pupils, personal and social skills may be an important prerequisite for learning. Areas such as personal care skills, managing own behaviour and managing their own emotions will be priorities for some pupils at different times (QCA 2001a).

Other skills such as ICT skills, working with others, and independence skills, may be equally important for some students in inclusive settings (Tod 1999). These cross-curricular and cross-*situational* targets will have relevance in all subjects, making it much more simple and effective both to address the targets and monitor progress. Cross-curricular targets give all staff a stake in helping the pupil to progress, and in celebrating achievement. There is no requirement to set IEP targets for all subjects of the secondary school curriculum. The targets must be directed at the skills or knowledge that the pupil most needs at any particular time.

The targets have to be realistic and understood by the pupil, the pupil's parents, teachers, and teaching assistants. It is advisable to keep targets simple, clear, and free of any jargon. Many parents will be reluctant to admit that they do not understand terminology used in IEPs. If they do not understand the IEP they will not be able to support their child. It is useful to write the IEP to the level of the understanding of the pupil. Ultimately it is the pupil who will achieve the targets, and it is the pupil who really needs to understand them. For some pupils this may mean using symbols to support the text, or having the targets spoken on audio tape, or signed and spoken on video.

Make sure that IEP targets are based upon what a pupil is expected to learn. It is surprising how many IEP targets are based on what teachers and teaching assistants will do, and so altogether bypass the pupil. Targets such as '*Dinesh will have access to an Alphasmart computer*' do not require the pupil to do or learn anything. Providing Dinesh with a computer may well be a laudable aspiration, but it is not an IEP target. '*Dinesh will save work on his Alphasmart after each lesson*' is a target towards which Dinesh can work over a limited period of time. He can be helped towards this target by staff in lessons, and by his parents for homework. When he learns to save his work after each lesson, he will have gained a valuable skill that can be developed and built on across the curriculum.

Annual review meetings

A pupil's Statement of Special Educational Needs is reviewed at the annual review meeting. This meeting, part of the statutory annual review process, involves the pupil, parents, the form tutor, the SENCO, and teaching assistants. Invitations are sent out to therapists working with the pupil, to educational psychologists, LEA officers, and sometimes the pupil's paediatrician. Even when these professionals are not able to attend the meeting often they send written reports giving a basis for future targets.

In addition to reviewing the statement, the annual review meeting will discuss the pupil's current IEP, and suggestions for new or amended targets can be made by those present. Those at the meeting sitting together as a team are able to identify the areas of greatest need for the pupil over the following twelve months. The IEP targets can then be based on these overarching, long-term targets. In this way, the overall shape of the individual education planning for the following year can be agreed and understood by all the key players. While the annual review meeting is separate from an IEP review, the opportunity of having pupil, parents, teachers, teaching assistants and professionals together is too good to miss. Linking long-term targets from the annual review to the short-term targets in the Individual Education Plan will ensure continuity, and limit the number of extra targets on which a pupil is working.

Once the long-term targets are agreed at the annual review, the SENCO or form teacher can then:

- set short-term targets;
- identify how the targets are to be addressed (resources, etc.);
- identify the school contexts in which the targets will be addressed (in-class, small group, one-to-one, etc.);
- identify staff members who will support the pupil in achieving the targets (peer support, teaching assistants, learning support service teachers, etc.);
- identify how parents can support the pupil to achieve the targets;
- arrange monitoring procedures.

Ensure targets are sufficiently sharp, clear, and unambiguous. The pupil should be able to go home and say,

'Guess what, Mum. Today I learned how to . . .', or, 'Today I learned that . . .'

Pupils and their parents will be involved in the process if targets are written in this way, and they will work together towards achieving the targets. For example, Dinesh, who has Down's Syndrome, has great difficulty remembering what equipment he needs to take to each lesson. He frequently gets into trouble for not having his pencil case, or the correct books. Dinesh identified this as an area he particularly wished to improve when he met with his form tutor to discuss his IEP targets. Therefore, based on his own assessment of his current needs, an appropriate IEP target for Dinesh could be, *'Dinesh will arrive at lessons with the books and equipment he needs'*. Systems could then be put into place to support Dinesh towards his achieving this target. A photographic cue card could be made for him, showing the resources needed for each day. A copy of this card could be kept at home, and his parents' role in the target could be to help Dinesh to pack his school bag each evening. Achieving this target would have a significant impact on Dinesh, in terms of his learning, his self-esteem, his independence, and in the way he is perceived by teachers.

Individual behaviour plans

Where pupils have behaviour problems in addition to learning difficulties, there is a danger that either the behaviour targets on the IEP will force out curricular targets, or that the pupil is given both an individual behaviour plan and an IEP. The pupil then ends up with more targets than he or she can manage, and little will be achieved. Keeping a balance of curricular and behaviour targets within the IEP gives a greater chance that the target setting will be successful. Behaviour difficulties often improve dramatically when IEP targets are realistic and understood by, and shared with, the pupil. Often, targets on individual behaviour plans are linked to a pupil's particular area of difficulty. For example, pupils with attention deficit hyperactivity disorder (ADHD) are often given targets relating to reducing their impulsivity or sitting still in class. For many pupils with ADHD such targets are not achievable and so have failure in-built.

Pupil involvement

When pupils are involved in setting their own targets and monitoring their own progress, teachers and parents find that the pupil tries harder, and is more motivated to succeed. Putting pupils at the heart of the target setting process gives them a stake in their own learning. Children with learning difficulties know what they find hard in school and they know what they want to improve. Surprisingly often their goals match those of the adults around them, but are frequently more ambitious. Spend time with the pupil before the annual review meeting, identifying strengths and concerns. This will clarify the target areas and prepare the pupil to speak out in the meeting. Such preparation is very important if pupils are to feel they have been heard. Annual review meetings are difficult enough for the professionals involved, let alone for pupils who should be supported and prepared in order to enable them to take a full part. Chapter 9 goes into more detail about pupil participation.

IEP targets from other professionals

Pupils with learning difficulties are frequently referred to other agencies. Health services (such as speech and language therapy, or physiotherapy, and occupational therapy), social services, or learning or behaviour support services, may well be involved with the child and his or her family. Incorporating targets from these agencies into a pupil's IEP can help teachers and therapists or support teachers to work together more effectively.

CASE STUDY | **Cara**

A pupil with an autistic spectrum disorder may be referred to the speech and language therapy service to develop social communication skills. Cara is in Year 8 and she has a diagnosis of Asperger Syndrome. In speech and language therapy she has been working on her understanding of metaphor. In discussion with the therapist, the SENCO suggests that this area could also be addressed in school as part of the IEP for the following term, as Cara's English set will be working on simile and metaphor.

Holistic IEPs that are written in conjunction with other agencies stand a much greater chance of being effective in helping the pupil achieve success. Sharing the responsibility in this way leavens the work of writing and monitoring IEPs. Collaborative working means that SENCOs and teachers do not feel isolated in dealing with the complexities of the SEN Code of Practice. Never dive alone!

Summary

The P scales are a rich resource for all schools, providing the small steps to success that support the inclusion of pupils with special educational needs. However, they are only a tool, and it is important to look at the whole child – strengths, talents, interests and special needs – when measuring progress. The P scales are also valuable as a source of targets for Individual Education Plans, showing progression that leads towards and into the National Curriculum.

In short, IEPs should

- be achievable and realistic;
- meet individual needs;
- have a time frame;
- be agreed with the pupil, parents and other professionals;
- shared with all staff who work with the student;
- celebrated when targets are achieved.

Chapter 7 looks at the social interaction and behaviour of pupils with learning difficulties.

Social interaction and behaviour

Social interaction

One of the major reasons for including pupils with learning difficulties in mainstream schools is the opportunity for social interaction. Among other children of the same age through the secondary school years, pupils gain good models of appropriate language and behaviour, and other pupils in the school learn about disability and become more accepting of diversity in society.

No-one can learn to interact merely by being in an occasional PSHE lesson, or in a small speech and language therapy group, although these classes and interventions will help to develop social skills to some extent. Pupils also need opportunities to try out what they have learned, and to get to know other people of the same age. As pupils move through the school they can become less tolerant of differences, and they may be embarrassed to have a person with a disability as a member of the social group. No school should accept this situation as simply inevitable, because it can be remedied. Chapter 3 gives details of how schools can intervene to help pupils develop social and interaction skills. A buddy system or Circle of Friends will provide a framework on which real relationships can develop. It is highly likely that such systems will need to be used more than once, depending on the individual pupil's changing level of interaction.

Pupils with learning difficulties sometimes may have hidden talents or interests that the school could use to develop interaction. A pupil may have an excellent singing voice, a love of painting, or be interested in computer games. Often school clubs are a great way to include pupils with learning difficulties in situations that guarantee success and interaction. There may be transport issues when clubs take place after school, but these problems should not be insurmountable.

CASE STUDY | **Saul**

Saul is in Year 10. Saul has a speech and language disorder and associated severe difficulties with literacy. His speech is very difficult to understand, and he spent much of Years 7 and 8 in the special needs unit of the school with little access to the mainstream curriculum. Frequently Saul was teased about his speech. The teasing was quite gentle but it bothered Saul deeply. He became increasingly withdrawn, and was reluctant to go outside the special needs unit.

By the time he reached Year 9, Saul had grown from a small boy to a tall, well built, young man. Physically he was very fit and had shone in the adapted games he played with the pupils from the special needs unit. The PE teacher invited Saul to join the Year 9 rugby squad for regular training. His talent for the game was obvious almost as soon as he ran onto the field. He trained twice each week, and by the end of the year he was playing for the Under 14 team. His speech difficulties mattered very little in the rugby team, and he socialised with the other players in school and in the evenings – much to his mother's concern. It was surprising how well he learned to sing the rugby songs on the coach to matches. His speech and his general abilities improved overall.

Behaviour

A pupil with learning difficulties very rarely has behaviour difficulties attributable directly to his or her learning disability. When pupils are offered age-appropriate activities at which they can succeed, behaviour difficulties will be kept to a minimum. As with all pupils, those with learning difficulties will behave the better in situations where they feel confident and valued. When the work they are expected to complete is far too complex – or far too easy – behaviour will deteriorate. Challenging behaviour is almost always the pupils' response to the demands made on them and on their environment. It is not necessarily an inherent problem within the pupil, or their disability (Jones 2002), but rather an indicator of how a pupil feels about school. When behaviour deteriorates suddenly there is always a reason. Impulsive or irrational behaviour occurs when pupils do not know what to do in a situation and is usually a sign of severe anxiety. Sending the pupil to stand outside the room, shouting, or exhortations to 'be good', will not be effective ways of dealing with the situation. It is important to look for the reason behind the behaviour and if possible address the cause of the problem. Observe the pupil in different lessons and at various times of the day. It is possible that, as with Jason in the example below, he is 'playing to the gallery' or copying others. Find out what is triggering the behaviour, and ask parents if they have noticed any changes at home.

CASE STUDY | **Jason**

Jason is in Year 9. He has a diagnosis of Fragile X Syndrome and this causes him to become anxious in noisy settings. During the fourth week of the school year Jason began to behave strangely in science. Either he bit his nails constantly and growled when anyone came near him, or he hopped around the room 'like a rabbit'. The science teacher reported these behaviours to the SENCO and Jason awaited assessment by the educational psychologist.

When the SENCO investigated Jason's behaviour, she found that he was in a bottom set for science. The majority of pupils in the class are boys who have statements of SEN for behavioural difficulties. These boys laughed at Jason when he misbehaved but he appeared to like the attention. The science teacher is in his second year of teaching. His lessons are not differentiated because the pupils are in sets for science. The teacher has never spoken directly to Jason.

The SENCO arranged for Jason to transfer to a higher science set with a more experienced teacher. This teacher worked with the SENCO to prepare differentiated activities. Jason worked with a partner or in small groups for each lesson, and was given praise by the teacher when he was on task. His behaviour and achievement improved immediately.

When there is more than one adult in a lesson, the teacher needs to be responsible (and to be seen by pupils to be so) for the learning and behaviour of all the pupils in the class, even those pupils supported one-to-one by a teaching assistant. Pupils are very quick to work out who has the authority in any situation, and will behave very differently for a teacher than they do for a teaching assistant.

The best way of learning why pupils use inappropriate behaviour is to observe them and identify 'flashpoints' – times in the school day when a pupil's behaviour becomes less appropriate. An ABC (Antecedents, Behaviours, and Consequences) assessment of situations can be undertaken, preferably by a colleague who does not currently teach the pupil, so remaining relatively dispassionate. This assessment should give a clearer understanding of the behaviours, and provide clues as to how to move forward.

Antecedents

Identify what has led up to the inappropriate behaviour. For example:

- Does the behaviour happen before or during some lessons more than others?
- Are particular pupils regularly involved?
- Could there be any sensory reasons for the behaviour (such as the noise of computers or a flickering fluorescent light)?

Behaviour

Describe the exact nature of the inappropriate behaviour.

- Be precise when describing behaviour as the differences may reflect differing reasons. For example, running out of class may be because the pupil is anxious or afraid, whereas running around the room may be to gain an adult's attention.

Consequences

Describe what happened as a consequence of the behaviour.

- How did the pupil react?
- How did other pupils react?
- How did the adults in the room react?
- Was the pupil punished? If so, how?
- Did the pupil receive the pay-off he or she wanted?
- Were there any longer-term consequences, such as parents being informed?

An ABC observation form can be found on the accompanying CD.

For many pupils, attention from adults is the need underlying the inappropriate behaviour. When children do not get the positive attention they need, they will make sure they get *some* attention – negative or positive – in the only way they know will work for certain; by using inappropriate behaviour. To ignore inappropriate behaviour really goes against the grain for teachers and teaching assistants. They feel that if they ignore the behaviour, the pupil is 'getting away with it' and that it is unfair to other pupils. But ignoring some behaviours does work – eventually. Other pupils usually are sufficiently aware to understand (without feeling that they have to try it too) that teachers are trying to change the inappropriate behaviour.

When a pupil's behaviour becomes either too dangerous or disruptive you will have to do something. The most effective course of action is to divert the pupil's attention. Ask him or her to do something for you, either in the classroom or in another part of the school. Changing the dynamics of a situation in this way will give the pupil a way out of a difficult situation, and usually restores order. Do not show that you are irritated or bothered by the behaviour. Stay emotionally neutral, with a calm voice and relaxed demeanour – very hard for a teacher to do when faced with challenging behaviour, but this is very important, and very effective. Anger management techniques may be appropriate for some pupils and information and advice can be sought from your LEA behaviour support team.

Behaviour prompt pictures/symbols can be effective to remind pupils of how they should behave. Symbols such as 'be quiet', 'wait' or 'sit down' can be held towards the pupil by the teacher or teaching assistant. This method is particularly useful where a teaching assistant is observing and supporting the whole class. The prompts can be used for any pupil who needs a reminder, and the cards do not necessarily require any additional comment or action. If symbols are used the pupils would need to learn their meanings, but they would then be useful for all children, including those with literacy difficulties.

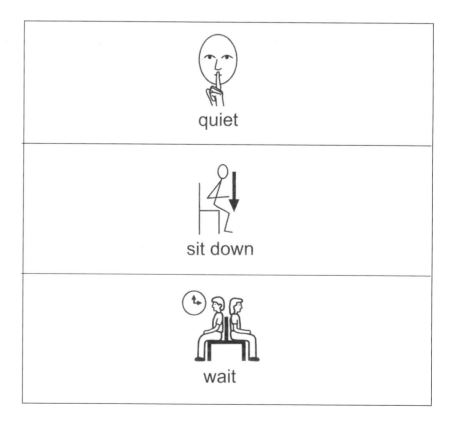

FIGURE 7.1 Behaviour prompt cards

Giving a pupil a message to take to another member of staff often works well: the school secretary is the ideal recipient for the note, mainly because the admin office is usually located close to the head teacher's office! Arrange beforehand that if the pupil arrives at the office with a piece of paper, he or she should be thanked and asked to wait for a few minutes. The pupil then is asked to return the note to the teacher. By the time the pupil returns the situation in the class will have been defused, and the other pupils will have settled down to work.

Pupils with learning difficulties rarely are given even small responsibilities, and just taking a note to the office will build up self-esteem. The pupil also has a break in concentration and gets a little physical exercise. Most pupils return to class having forgotten the previous difficulties. A teaching assistant could escort the pupil to the office, or other classroom, but it is better if they go alone. The teaching assistant could shadow the pupil from a distance if there are any safety concerns. Dealing with disruptive behaviour in this way causes minimal disruption for the teacher, the class, or the individual pupil. It also helps teachers to feel they are not alone in tackling disruptive behaviour, and encourages cooperation between colleagues.

Wherever possible ignore low-level aggravation. Instead, accentuate and praise anything that is positive. This does take time to work, but will have the desired effect in the end. Minimise the language used when giving praise, so that the pupil knows exactly what was good behaviour. Phrases such as 'Good listening', 'Good watching' or 'Neat writing' are perfect when said with a smile. Pupils eventually learn which behaviours are acceptable and which are not. This 'shower of affirmation' approach is very powerful, and will transform a child's behaviour.

It is always worth trying to accentuate the positive because the alternative is the 'he or she mustn't get away with it' approach, with a stream of corrections and reprimands. Reprimands quickly lose effect when a pupil constantly is being told off, getting the attention they crave – albeit negative attention. The situation then escalates with the pupil becoming an increasing nuisance in classes and needing increasingly severe sanctions. This situation is in no-one's interest, and only serves to make teachers and teaching assistants stressed, and the pupil with learning difficulties unhappy and confused.

Some schools provide training for staff in positive physical intervention/ restraint. Restraint is only necessary with very few pupils in equally few situations, usually following badly-handled confrontations with pupils. Where adults do not feel able to 'back down' so that a pupil does not 'get the upper hand', there can be no winners. People with learning difficulties very rarely are deliberately vindictive or aggressive.

There will inevitably be occasions when behaviour goes beyond low-level aggravation and some form of verbal chastisement is needed. The correction should take place immediately, but in any case as soon as possible after the incident has occurred. If you wait until the end of the lesson, or even the end of the day, the pupil will have forgotten what happened and will not understand why they are being chastised. Simple language and short phrases immediately expressed will be much more effective. When angry our vocal tone rises, we speak more quickly, and use more complex words and sentence structures including irony and sarcasm. Pupils who have comprehension difficulties, which category includes almost all children with learning difficulties, will not understand what is being said. These pupils will actively switch off, with the speech becoming simply a wash of sound.

Use a form of words that condemns the inappropriate behaviour rather than the child, such as, 'Don't tear pages from your book. If you need spare paper, get it from my desk.' Being told that they are 'naughty' or 'bad' does not help pupils to change behaviours and can seriously damage self-esteem, confidence and motivation. Tell the pupil what they did that was wrong, and then tell them what they should have done; when they know how to behave there will be a greater likelihood of future compliance.

Before beginning to tell them off, wherever possible take the pupil to a private place. Dressing-down a pupil in public should be a thing of the past, especially for someone with learning difficulties who may react in a less mature way. Embarrassment will make the pupil less motivated in lessons and less willing to interact with peers.

Make your requirements explicit to the pupil. Let the pupil know exactly how you expect them to behave; what they *should* do in the situation. All teachers have slightly different expectations of pupil behaviour. For example, pupils can talk in some subjects but not in others, and what does 'talking quietly' mean? Teachers may need to repeat many times their own expectations. Social norms, such as holding doors open for others, that most people take for granted, may not be known or understood by pupils with learning difficulties. These norms will need to be taught explicitly.

Moving around school between lessons is a complex and challenging situation, both socially and intellectually. Holding the door open may be the last thing on the pupil's mind, and may simply be forgotten. Show the pupil how to hold the door open, and explain when it should be closed. Something this simple frequently causes pupils with learning difficulties to be in trouble with teachers or prefects, but they usually have no idea what they have done to cause them to be told off or punished.

Rules

Pupils with learning difficulties generally like to obey school rules. In order to follow rules, pupils have to know and understand them. When rules are clear and unambiguous they give a sense of structure and order. School rules usually are written down in a prospectus or in homework planners and for most pupils that is sufficient. Other pupils however will need opportunities to learn the school rules, and time to discuss them with an adult. Only when this has been done should pupils with learning difficulties be expected to know and obey school rules.

Some pupils need to have additional, individual rules that will help them manage their own behaviour in situations they find difficult. A pupil with learning difficulties may not know such things as:

- hands must be raised before speaking to the teacher;
- do not run in corridors;
- money is needed to buy a snack;
- ask before borrowing someone else's rubber or ruler.

A few specific personal rules can be written down in the pupil's planner. The rules can be shared with a teaching assistant or pupil mentor in registration and form periods. The pupil's parents and all subject teachers will need to have a copy. These individual rules frequently can deflect potential misdemeanours, yet they take little time and effort to put in place. When the pupil knows and understands what is expected, he or she can then be subject to the usual school sanctions.

Offer practical alternatives when unacceptable behaviour is repeated. For example, when a pupil always throws the pen down onto the desk, provide a desk tidy where the pen can be placed. Such a simple action often can defuse a potentially explosive situation. Dealing with the quantity of 'stuff' they have with them can be overwhelming for some pupils. Those with an autistic spectrum disorder may spend much of a lesson setting out all their pens, felt-tips, rubbers, rulers, protractor, set square, etc. – and this in geography! It is not that the pupil wants to do this, but they do not know what equipment is important for each different lesson, and so everything comes out and has to be placed in the right order. A simple list of words, symbols or small photographs kept in each classroom can very quickly solve the problem.

Where a pupil uses several unacceptable behaviours in school, attempt to change only one behaviour at a time. Tell the pupil what needs to change, and teach an acceptable alternative. Make regular notes on the changes in the pupil's behaviour. This may seem like excessive record keeping, but when teachers and teaching assistants can see a pupil making improvements in behaviour, they begin to feel better about both themselves and the pupil. Without noting down the changes it can be easy to miss genuine improvements in a pupil's behaviour. Any improvements should be celebrated with the pupil, and with their parents, and amongst staff. Changing staff perceptions of a pupil is often as important as changing the pupil's behaviour. 'Once a nuisance always a nuisance' can be the attitude – even when the pupil's behaviour has improved dramatically.

Whole-staff understanding

Where there are adults in the school who do not understand the reasons for a pupil's behaviour, a negative or angry response from just one adult can cause a pupil great distress. Pupils with learning difficulties often will have no behaviour difficulties in class, but may experience conflicts with other pupils at lunchtimes or breaks. It requires a high level of understanding and skill to manage such situations. Lunchtime supervisors, administrators or cleaning staff rarely have specific training in behaviour management and usually have to rely on their own experiences of school or of raising children. Inappropriate management can cause minor arguments to become major incidents.

The following case study is an example.

CASE STUDY	Chrissie

Chrissie is in Year 8. She has Down's Syndrome. There was a disturbance on Chrissie's lunch table. The lunchtime supervisor, Mrs Jones, went over to investigate the problem. She saw Chrissie rocking in her seat and repeatedly trying to take a chocolate bar from the boy sitting next to her. Mrs Jones told Chrissie to stop rocking, and to leave the boy alone. Chrissie stood up and began to cry and shout. Mrs Jones took hold of her arm and encouraged her to sit down again, and to continue eating. At this Chrissie lashed out and again grabbed at the chocolate bar the boy was now eating. In lashing out she struck Mrs Jones on the face. Mrs Jones was clearly shocked and upset, and shouted at Chrissie who then tried to run out of the hall. A teacher and a teaching assistant restrained Chrissie before she could leave the hall. She fell to the floor and refused to get up. The two adults then spent the next hour sitting on the dining hall floor trying unsuccessfully to calm Chrissie down. Eventually her mother was called, and she went home.

Chrissie arrived back in school the next day and behaved as if nothing had happened.

The original commotion at the table was because the boy next to Chrissie had 'swapped' his biscuit for her chocolate bar. She had used her limited language skills to ask for it back. The boy had refused and the whole table was laughing at Chrissie's response of rocking and grabbing at the chocolate bar. When reprimanded by Mrs Jones, Chrissie had become really upset. Chrissie is tactile defensive – she does not like being touched. When Mrs Jones took her arm she reacted instinctively because of her emotional state, and lashed out. She had not meant to harm Mrs Jones, but when shouted at, her instinct had been to get away from the situation as quickly as possible. When stopped and held by two adults the sensory overload was too great for Chrissie and she then dropped to the floor, curling into the foetal position. This was not Chrissie behaving badly – it was a survival technique.

In this situation Chrissie did not know what she had done wrong, nor did she understand why Mrs Jones was angry. The comment in the incident book notes that Chrissie's behaviour was violent and aggressive and that she needed to be restrained. The boy who enjoyed her chocolate bar also enjoyed the entertainment.

If training had been given before Chrissie arrived at the school this situation would more likely have been sensitively handled. Mrs Jones would have known that Chrissie did not like to be touched, and recognised her rocking as a sign of anxiety. Harness the skills of lunchtime supervisors, administration staff, and even the caretaker, and this will pay dividends by minimising escalating behaviours in less structured school settings.

Safe havens

Many schools are now creating safe havens for vulnerable pupils. This may be a room or an area in the school where pupils can choose to go at break and lunchtimes to stay safe, keep out of trouble, calm down, or just to catch up on work. It is vital that the safe haven is staffed by experienced teachers and teaching assistants. Safe havens are often valuable in giving support to pupils with learning difficulties, and those with behaviour problems. Pupils can prepare for the next lessons, or get support for homework. Often computer suites or SEN bases are used for this purpose. Here the resources needed are minimal; a few board-games, paper and pens, and books are all that are really necessary. The staff member is the most important resource, and being on duty in the safe haven is usually a pleasant experience.

Equal and realistic expectations

Do make sure that you have realistic expectations of how a pupil with learning difficulties should and could behave. Each child has their own personality traits and quirks which may annoy others. Some pupils with learning difficulties have physical tics that they cannot control. Some pupils hum quietly – or not so quietly – when they are concentrating. Others may make noises intermittently or have stereotypical behaviours, such as turning around before they sit down. These individual traits will need to be taken into account before a pupil's behaviour can be described as disruptive.

Pupils with learning difficulties are watched much more closely than other pupils because they have special educational needs. Teachers and teaching assistants make sure they stay on task throughout lessons. Most pupils *without* learning difficulties attend only intermittently; sometimes listening or working; other times looking out of the window or chatting to a friend. Be sure not to expect higher standards of behaviour from pupils with learning difficulties than expected from other students. Observations by colleagues are a valuable source of information on really how well a pupil is performing in lessons. Monitoring the time that all pupils stay on task will give a more accurate picture of how hard the pupil with learning difficulties is working in comparison with others.

Can't or won't

Teachers are great communicators, very skilled in speaking to and with pupils, and in assessing their moods and intentions. Knowing whether a pupil is unable to do work or is simply refusing to try is always difficult to determine. Teachers gauge the pupil's response from what they say, how they say it, from eye contact, from facial expression, and from body language. All this information, combined with previous knowledge of the pupil's work, determines the teacher's response. Is the pupil to be given extra help, or a detention?

It is less straightforward with pupils with learning difficulties. They may appear to be refusing to attempt the work, or to be taking an inordinately long time over it. It may be impossible for the pupil to say why the work has not been done. Often pupils with learning difficulties smile at the teacher when asked why they haven't finished work. This can be misconstrued as defiance or plain rudeness. The pupil probably is really perplexed. The teacher is someone the pupil likes, and so when the teacher speaks, the pupil smiles. At this point the pupil is probably not listening to the words spoken by the teacher, but looking at the facial expression. When the teacher becomes angry or gives a detention the pupil often has no idea of the reason. Eye contact, facial expression, and body language, are not likely to be sufficiently sophisticated to transmit such complex feelings deliberately. In this situation misunderstandings are common, and lead to distress on all sides.

'Manipulative' pupils?

Teachers frequently report that pupils with learning difficulties are 'manipulative'. When investigated, this adjective is found to mean that the pupil wants to get their own way. If this was the case then the pupil with learning difficulties is no different from any other pupil. All children want their own way. As they grow, children learn that they have to wait or conform to adult requests. They still want their own way, but most also want to please adults. Pupils with learning difficulties take longer to learn this particular social skill. They may not necessarily want to please a particular adult and are likely to have access only to more immature strategies.

CASE STUDY	Sian

Sian is in Year 9 and has an autistic spectrum disorder. She loves all lessons, except Mrs Phillips' design and technology classes. She finds the noises of the machines very frightening, but has so far managed to remain relatively calm, and has stayed in the lessons. For the past three weeks, however, Sian has used a number of tactics firstly not to go to the lesson, and secondly as often as possible to get out of the workshop. The first week Sian said she had a headache and was allowed to stay in the library. On the second week she asked six times to go to the toilet. On the third occasion Sian kept returning to her form room, saying she had forgotten various items of equipment, her pen, her design folder, etc.

The teaching assistant in the science department realised that something was wrong and spoke to Sian at dinner time. When the teaching assistant mentioned the workshop Sian immediately began to cry. Mrs Phillips arranged for a small group including Sian to work in another room on the weeks when the machines were in use. Sian's behaviour gradually improved, and she will now tolerate some noise in the workshops.

Tiredness

In order to understand and respond to lessons in school, pupils with learning difficulties have to work very hard. The effort they expend will be greater than almost any other pupil in the class. Once most pupils learn a routine they hardly need to think about it, whereas pupils with learning difficulties need to think about almost everything, every time. They can take little for granted. This is another reason why visual cues and lists are so useful. They need to remember and actively think about such things as how to get to the next lesson, the equipment they will need for each activity, and catching the school bus home. This constant active thinking, in addition to the school work and the effort of social interaction, causes pupils with learning difficulties to become very tired by the end of the school day.

Tiredness will also have an impact on the amount and quality of homework that pupils with learning difficulties will be able to complete. If parents report that their child is becoming anxious about homework, consider setting less or give the pupil a time extension. Teachers will get the best during the school day from pupils with learning difficulties if those pupils have had a chance to rest during the previous evening. Homework clubs held immediately after school can be a useful support, and staff will be better able to gauge whether a pupil really is too tired to do the homework, or is just reluctant to work. When pupils are genuinely too tired to complete homework, provide them with something else to do at home, whether collecting objects, reading a passage, or listening to information on a tape. It is important that other pupils do not see that a fellow pupil is 'getting away with' homework, and the pupil with learning difficulties needs to keep up a pattern of working at home.

The impact of illness on behaviour

As with all pupils, the behaviour of pupils with learning difficulties will change when they have an illness. Unfortunately it is not possible to anticipate how the behaviour will change. Some pupils become very withdrawn and quiet, others have the opposite reaction. Try always to investigate to find out if illness could be the cause of negative changes in a pupil's behaviour. Often a telephone call to parents will answer concerns before a difficult situation develops in school.

CASE STUDY	Jackson

Jackson is in Year 7 and has severe learning difficulties. He usually behaves well in school, but he is sometimes wilful and can refuse to do as he is asked.

At the start of the spring term Jackson's behaviour deteriorated rapidly. He became increasingly resistant to requests to work, and he was verbally and physically abusive to the teachers, teaching assistants, and other pupils. Jackson's behaviour was also very challenging at home, especially as he no longer slept through the night. He appeared unhappy and anxious. His parents put his behaviour down to the hormonal changes of puberty. In the week before half-term Jackson kicked and injured a teacher's leg. In line with school policy, Jackson was given a temporary exclusion, and several teachers and parents lobbied the governors to have him removed from the school permanently.

Jackson's parents were very concerned and so took him to see the family doctor. The doctor discovered that Jackson had a very serious ear infection that would have caused him continual discomfort. He was given antibiotics and after a few days his behaviour returned to normal.

Jackson did not have the language skills to express the pain he was experiencing. His only way of showing the distress was through his behaviour.

This case study is not to condone Jackson's behaviour, but to explain why the incidents occurred.

Medication

Some pupils with learning difficulties need to take medicines for conditions such as epilepsy. It may take several months for doctors to perfect the choice and dosage of medication for a particular individual, and the pupil's behaviour is likely to be erratic during this time. Communication with parents is obviously of vital importance in this situation, and school staff will need to be understanding and more tolerant of unusual behaviour.

Potential difficulties in non-directed time

Most pupils with learning difficulties quickly learn how to behave in lessons. They become familiar and comfortable in the structured settings, and behave accordingly. Problems frequently arise in less structured times in school, such as the transitions between lessons, breaks and lunchtimes. The problems often arise because of misunderstandings between students, or because the pupil does not know what they are expected to do and how they should behave. During breaks, the buddy system or Circle of Friends (see Chapter 3) will support pupils with learning difficulties. Members of the Circle of Friends inviting the pupil to join games in the playground, or talking to him or her, will often make the world of difference to a pupil's behaviour and confidence.

In breaks and lunchtimes do not assign a teaching assistant to accompany a pupil with learning difficulties. An adult trailing round serves only to make the pupil appear more different to other pupils, and makes interaction much less likely. However, the extra teaching assistant could join other staff on the rota for the safe haven. This use of support hours would be preferable and far more effective than having the teaching assistant shepherd the pupil in the playground. Some head teachers refer to one-to-one teaching assistants as 'minders' and sometimes it is easy to see why.

Problems in unstructured times are the most difficult to resolve because it is that very lack of structure that causes some pupils to behave inappropriately. Pupils with learning difficulties need three elements of structure to be in place. These elements are:

- social
- physical
- time.

Social

It may be that the pupil with learning difficulties cannot cope with the social demands of breaks. Lining up to buy a drink, trying to join a game, or returning a library book, involves meeting and interacting with many people, adults and pupils. The pupil has to remember how to address and respond to each different person. A number of such fleeting interactions in a short period of time can overload a pupil, cause anxiety or overexcitement, and lead to inappropriate behaviour. Limiting the social demands will help pupils, especially when they are new to the school. For example, the drink or snack could be paid for by parents in advance, and the pupil could collect it from the tuck shop without queuing. Once again, the buddy group or Circle of Friends offers support and provides a consistent friendly face.

Problems arise when pupils with learning difficulties copy the behaviours of other pupils in less appropriate ways. This is the case especially when they copy the physical play of younger children.

Physical

Secondary schools are large and complex communities: different buildings with different purposes, but frequently without signs. Signs with words and symbols will help both pupils and visitors find their way around independently. Outside areas often are even more confusing – large open areas without demarcations. They often adjoin the school field without a fence or other boundary. This space

CASE STUDY   Mandev

Mandev is in Year 8. He has a diagnosis of Asperger Syndrome. He spends most breaks walking around the edge of the play area or sitting on the steps. In recent days he has been in trouble for 'assaulting' other pupils and a teaching assistant. These unprovoked attacks (as they were described in the school incident book) took the form of Mandev jumping onto the back of his 'victim' and hanging on until forcibly removed.

Fortunately, Mandev's classmate had seen several of the incidents and he suggested that his form teacher go outside to see for himself. The boy had observed that Mandev's behaviour happened after he had been watching a group of boys play. The game consisted of a boy jumping onto a friend's back and being swung around to cause him to fall off. The rest of the group cheered them on.

Mandev had watched the game and had seen how the boys enjoyed themselves. He copied their game because he wanted to have fun. He did not understand that he should have asked if the other pupils –mostly girls – wanted to play the game, and he certainly could not understand why everyone was so angry with him.

is wonderful for most pupils because they have the freedom to run around and play football, etc., but that very space can cause huge anxieties for some pupils with learning difficulties. They may want to run but will not know when to stop, and so then could go outside the school boundary (and break another school rule in the process).

Some pupils with learning difficulties can become distressed in very cold or very hot weather, and so may behave inappropriately. Physically they may not be able to regulate their body temperature, or they may be unable to match their clothing to the weather conditions.

Most of these problems can be avoided by giving the pupil with learning difficulties something to do during break times: going to choir; helping in the office; joining a board game or art club; or reading in the library. Activities such as these will avoid outside behaviour difficulties and will support the pupil's developing social skills.

Time

Pupils with learning difficulties may not have a complete understanding of time. Breaks on a freezing day are bearable because we know that we can go back into the warmth in fifteen minutes. Most pupils know how long fifteen minutes lasts, and they use that sense of time to anticipate when the bell will ring. Pupils with learning difficulties may not have that ability, and for them that cold break could go on forever. They cannot anticipate the end of unpalatable situations, and so behave in the way most likely to make the situation stop. By behaving inappropriately, they get to go inside, where social, physical and temporal boundaries are much clearer.

Structuring lunchtimes and breaks will give pupils the support they need. A picture or symbol timetable is often all that is needed. The timetable gives a temporal framework to the unstructured time, and also tells the pupil what to do. The timetable can be in words and/or symbols and should be set out to cover either each day or a week, depending on the level of understanding of the pupil.

The following timetable is for Siobhan in Year 10. She is on first sitting for dinner on Monday, Tuesday and Wednesday, but on second sitting on Thursday and Friday. This causes her huge problems as frequently she goes into the wrong sitting, and becomes distressed when told that she has to wait. This timetable is reviewed every two weeks. The timetable was drawn up by Siobhan and a teaching assistant. Siobhan chose the activities and when she wanted to do them.

Day	Break	Dinner	
Monday	Computer	Canteen	Library
Tuesday	Board games	Canteen	Choir
Wednesday	Library	Canteen	Art club
Thursday	Computer	Office	Canteen
Friday	Band	Library	Canteen

Clock faces can be added to the timetable to let pupils know when to go to clubs or back to class. More information and/or symbols might be added depending on the understanding of the individual pupil.

The vocabulary of feelings

In order to effect changes in our behaviour we need to be able to think about, and understand, why we behave in certain ways. Underpinning that understanding is a rich vocabulary of words relating to emotions. We have access to a wonderfully rich and complex language through which we express and consider our feelings in precise detail. Adolescent girls in particular spend much of their free time discussing how they feel, and how other people make them feel. They pick up on unspoken cues from other people, and give friends emotional support by empathising with their problems.

The limited language that is available to pupils with learning difficulties denies them the full ability to reflect and think through the reasons for their own behaviours. These pupils do not have an understanding of how their behaviour makes other people feel.

Schools need to build opportunities into the curriculum so that pupils with learning difficulties may develop a wider vocabulary of feelings. These do not have to be taught separately from other subjects, but the pupil's key worker could check that all opportunities available are maximised. For example, in Year 9 history, lessons on the French Revolution can include discussions on how the peasants felt when they were cold and hungry; how the aristocracy felt when they were in hiding, etc., and the words used could then be recorded in a book or on disk and reviewed in the regular mentor session.

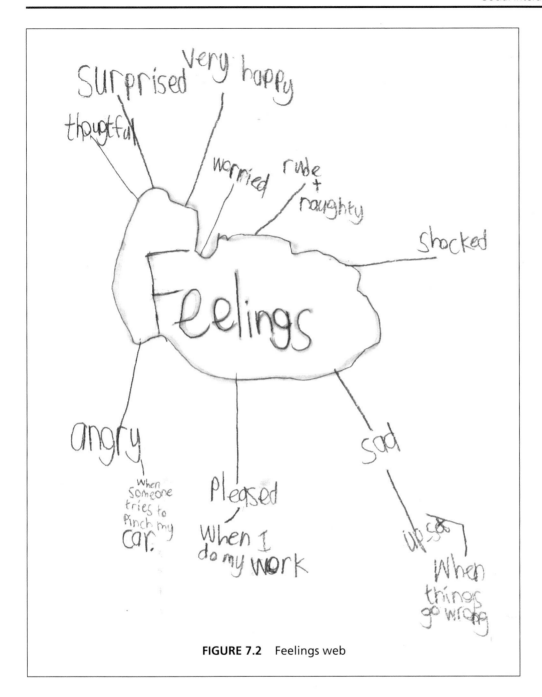

FIGURE 7.2 Feelings web

Social stories

Social stories can be written by an adult who knows the pupil well. The story helps the pupil to understand situations they find difficult. They let the pupil know what to expect and explain how to behave. This approach is based on the social stories method devised by Carol Gray (1994a). Social stories should be short, and may include photographs, drawings and/or symbols. The story needs to give the pupil information about where and when the situation occurs, who is involved, what usually happens and why (Jones 2002). Sometimes reading just two or three sentences regularly with the pupil can prompt changes in understanding and behaviour.

| Box 7.1 | **Example of a social story** |

At break times most children go outside to play. When it has been raining, we all have to stay on the concrete area. This is because the grass gets muddy and makes our shoes and clothes dirty. My mum feels annoyed when my clothes get muddy. I will stay on the concrete area at break times. Mrs Williams or Mrs Smith will tell me when I can go on the grass.

Summary

Inappropriate or challenging behaviour is the major reason for the breakdown in placements for pupils with learning difficulties in mainstream secondary schools. Yet the problems are rarely within the pupil, but caused mostly by inflexible or inappropriate school systems. Schools must adapt to meet more diverse needs – diverse in terms of learning styles and behaviour – in order to cater for greater diversity amongst pupils. Taking time to observe and talk to the individual pupil to find the underlying causes of the behaviour will often throw up relatively simple and practical solutions.

The changes in pupils' learning, social and emotional needs in Years 10 and 11 will present new challenges and opportunities. These are explored in Chapter 8.

Key Stage 4 . . . and beyond

Key Stage 4 is the time when students with learning difficulties really can concentrate on developing the skills they will need both for post-16 education and for an independent adult life. Students need a curriculum delivered in the context of the school and other settings that provides a combination of basic skills and independent living skills. Nationally recognised qualifications are now available that enable recognition and celebration of the small steps of achievement made by students with learning difficulties. These qualifications give a springboard for their future. This does not mean a school has to create a new curriculum for each student. Much of the learning will take place within GCSE classes, and the remainder of the time will be spent in smaller groups together with other students also taking alternative accredited courses.

The end of Key Stage 3 frequently heralds concerns about how to accommodate the needs of one or two pupils with learning difficulties in a curriculum designed for pupils taking GCSE examination courses. The 'special school option' is raised at the Year 9 Transition Review, often because it is easier to move a student to a special school than to set up appropriate provision within the mainstream. Even a strong parental determination for a student to continue in mainstream can be broken down at this point in the face of overwhelming negativity from a school. This is a great disservice to the student and perpetuates the status quo, where good GCSE results are seen as the measure of an effective school. While it is GCSE results that count in the national league tables, so acting as a guarantee for the future success of a school, it is a strong head teacher who, in Key Stage 4, can and will stand up for the inclusion of pupils with learning difficulties. League tables are a powerful disincentive for schools to include students with learning difficulties at Key Stage 4. Some schools have made the 14 to 16 curriculum accessible to all, proving that schools which are truly inclusive are good schools for all students. Excellent GCSE results can be achieved alongside excellent vocational and entry level course results. Good schools are about much more than GCSE results. Good schools respond to the strengths, talents and needs of all students.

The first step towards success at Key Stage 4 is not to worry as the end of Year 9 approaches. If a pupil with learning difficulties has made adequate progress in Key Stage 3, and is a full and happy member of the school community, there is no reason why he or she should not do equally well in Key Stage 4. Fortunately there has been a sea change in attitude towards curricular opportunities for all students between the ages of 14 and 19 years. More appropriate vocational and life skills courses are now available that can be tailored to meet individual priorities within a group context. There remain problems for those secondary schools with small cohorts of pupils needing an alternative curriculum at Key Stage 4.

Such problems can be overcome by linking with other schools, and by using a little creative thinking. In these ways schools can better share resources and expertise. Collaboration and partnerships with neighbouring schools enable the offer of a wider spread of courses appropriate to students' interests and abilities. Links with local further education colleges and colleges of technology will further widen the range of provision for all students. For students with learning difficulties this is especially the case. Further education colleges run part-time courses in an interesting range of subjects which can be accessed by pupils in Years 10 and 11. Sampling new skills such as bricklaying, painting and decorating, word processing, horticulture, and catering, will open up new horizons and may reveal hidden talents. Working in a new, more adult, environment will also develop personal, social and communication skills in a new context.

Consider possible links with a local special school. All special schools with secondary departments offer accredited courses for their students. Invite the local special schools to combine their accredited courses with those on offer in the mainstream. Where only one or two students need to access alternative qualifications, their work can be assessed by a special school that is a centre for the awarding body.

The widening gap

Many schools worry how they will offer appropriate courses to students with learning difficulties in Key Stage 4 when the difference in ability levels is so great. The widening ability gap can seem stretched to breaking point, with no obvious points of contact with the GSCE framework. Concentrating on the ability gap, and comparing the attainment of a student with learning difficulties with that of chronological peers, is totally counter-productive. Accept the difference and move on. Pupils with learning difficulties will not catch up with their peers, but they will make progress appropriate to their level of ability and understanding, and sometimes will achieve far more than is thought possible. We must celebrate every small achievement every bit as much as we celebrate five A to Cs at GCSE.

Complete GCSE courses will not be appropriate for students with learning difficulties, but there will be elements of those courses accessible as part of other accredited schemes. In Year 9, take a hard look at the learning strengths and needs of the pupil with learning difficulties. Identify where those strengths and needs can match the GCSE syllabus in each subject. Some pupils with learning difficulties may have talents in practical subjects, such as technology, music or art. They may not be able to complete the theoretical aspects of the subjects, but they might join in with the more practical elements. That practical work can then be used as evidence for alternative accreditation, and be included in the pupil's progress folder.

Disapplication

Disapplication is the process by which schools can withdraw a student from some National Curriculum subjects. Individual students can be disapplied from National Curriculum subjects through their Statement of Special Educational Needs. The flexibility available in the revised 14 to 16 curriculum that comes into force in September 2004 should be explored before a school considers disapplying a student. The Inclusion Statement in the National Curriculum documents gives additional advice on including students with a diverse range of ability. The revised Key Stage 4 curriculum is designed to give schools sufficient flexibility to meet the needs of all students.

Entitlement areas

From September 2004 a new category of entitlement curriculum areas will be introduced. These entitlement areas are:

- the arts
- design and technology
- the humanities
- modern foreign languages.

Entitlement areas are designed to give schools greater flexibility in curriculum design and so the better to meet the needs of individual students. Schools will no longer be required to teach design and technology and modern foreign languages to all students. However, schools will be required to ensure that design and technology and modern foreign languages are available to any student wishing to study them. There are similar entitlements to study the arts and the humanities.

These changes mean that disapplication of the National Curriculum at Key Stage 4 through a Statement of Special Educational Needs will be unnecessary. Individual needs for all students can be addressed through entry level courses linked to National Curriculum English and maths. Personal, social, life and work skills can be taught through a combination of appropriate modules from accredited courses, inclusion in National Curriculum lessons, and work experience.

Where students with learning difficulties are included in GCSE lessons, it will still be necessary for the teacher to differentiate the activities to make them relevant to the needs of the individual student.

In the case study below, Jasmir is working towards qualifications on an ASDAN programme. ASDAN (Award Scheme Development and Accreditation Network) is an approved awarding body offering programmes that combine activity based curriculum enrichment with a framework for the development of key skills and life skills.

CASE STUDY | **Jasmir**

Jasmir is in Year 10. He has severe learning difficulties. Jasmir's curriculum plan for Year 10 is based on the ASDAN Bronze Challenge Award. He is taught some lessons in a small group of ten students, all of whom are working on either the Bronze or Silver Challenge awards. He also is included in some lessons with his form group, and with various sets for other subjects. He works in his form group for citizenship, PSHE, sex education, PE and games, and religious education; in GCSE lessons for practical music, art and drama; and in the ASDAN group for communication and literacy skills, maths, ICT, humanities, and careers. This variety of groups means that Jasmir can maintain relationships with his form group, but also meet new students in the various sets and form new relationships with students in the ASDAN group.

Jasmir no longer has one-to-one support in lessons. The teaching assistants now work with the whole group or set. Although he still has transport to and from school, Jasmir is expected to make his own way to lessons, on time, and with the appropriate equipment. Jasmir has a range of visual supports to help him to be more independent, and difficulties arise only when there is an unforeseen change in plans.

At his Year 9 transition review, Jasmir told of his wish to work at his local Sikh temple. He now spends one afternoon each week at the temple doing a variety of jobs. At the start of Year 10 he was supported in work experience by a teaching assistant from school, but a taxi now takes him to the temple at lunchtime, and he walks the few hundred yards to his home at the end of the day.

Planning for Key Stage 4

There should be a sense of real freedom when schools begin to plan for pupils with learning difficulties in Key Stage 4. For once, a pupil is not being fitted into the system but the system can be adapted and shaped to fit the pupil.

The revised Key Stage 4 allows schools the flexibility to make adaptations possible without the need to create a separate curriculum for a small number of pupils. The 14 to 16 curriculum is now sufficiently flexible to include vocational and life skills courses alongside GCSE. The changes have been designed to enable schools to offer programmes the better to meet individual needs and the strengths of all students (QCA 2003).

Planning for Key Stage 4 needs to begin at the start of Year 9, in order for the school to have time to set in place the appropriate courses. There are two key meetings at the end of Key Stage 3 that together ensure the needs of pupils and the wishes of their parents are met: the Guidance interview, and the Transition Review.

The Guidance interview

This interview should take place towards the end of Year 9, by which time the pupil will need to have received appropriate preparation and advice on the choices he or she will have to make. Preparation must be handled carefully in order to elicit the true feelings and wishes of the student. This is especially important for pupils with restricted communication skills. While many pupils will be able to complete simple questionnaires with adult help, others will need to use symbol-supported text, signing, or oral methods, to get across their views. (Chapter 9 gives advice on how to work with students to help them give their views on their education and future.)

Guidance interviews give an opportunity to discuss with an impartial and informed adult the pupil's aspirations for future education and training. This adult can be a member of the school staff, or a personal adviser from the Connexions service. Advice and guidance will be given regarding the curriculum plan for Key Stage 4, and the implications of the plan for the student's education in the post-16 phase. Priorities for the curriculum plan for Key Stage 4 can be agreed and drafted in outline at this interview, and so may be circulated with reports, be discussed at the annual review of statement in Year 9, and be included in the transition planning process.

The Key Stage 4 curriculum plan

This planning document will form part of the student's Transition Plan. The document needs to be tightly focused, and created with, and agreed by, the student.

The curriculum plan for Key Stage 4 should specify:

- the student's strengths;
- any particular educational needs;
- the student's ambitions for Key Stage 4 and post-16 education;
- parents' views and aspirations;
- the school's agreed responses by means of courses and subject options.

Figures 8.1a and b are pages 1 and 2 of Jasmir's Key Stage 4 curriculum plan. A blank version of Figures 8.1a and b are on the accompanying CD.

The Transition Review

The Transition Review is the annual statement review for a student in Year 9. This review meeting must discuss the issues relating to the student's transition from school to post-school education and into adult life. The review must involve the student, parents, and the Connexions service. Social services must be invited, together with any other agencies likely to play a significant role in the student's life during post-school years.

Most students will be keen to attend the meeting and to express their own preferences and views, but will need help to prepare. The student must know in advance what will happen and what is expected of them. For more vulnerable students, the opportunity to speak first in the meeting, and then to leave, will be more suitable. Students not wishing to attend in person could record their views on video tape that may then be played to the meeting.

Following the meeting a personal adviser from the Connexions service will usually draw up a Transition Plan. The Transition Plan draws together information from people in the school and from other agencies, and creates a coherent plan for the young person in their transition to adult life. It will cover school provision at Key Stage 4 as well as post-school arrangements. The curriculum plan for Key Stage 4 is an important element of the Transition Plan, and will set out how the curriculum will enable the student to develop new educational, personal and vocational skills. Setting the curriculum plan into the wider context of the Transition Plan will ensure the curriculum is more responsive, and is more relevant to the longer-term needs of the student.

Work-related learning

Most people take for granted the ability to work for one's living and to be part of, and contribute to, the community in which one lives. This is not the case for the majority of adults with learning difficulties. To get up on time, and to go out to work; having to be punctual; negotiating public transport; working by different rules and with different people, these are all skills that everyone needs to develop. Work-related learning is now a statutory requirement for Key Stage 4. Work-related learning is not a new subject; rather it is a context used to develop knowledge, skills and understanding that will be useful in employment. Work-

Key Stage 4 Curriculum Plan	Name: Jasmir S.	Year 10/Year 11
English: Communication Skills (ASDAN group and SALT) Literacy for Life (ASDAN group)	**Arts, Design and Technology:** ASDAN: Expressive arts Inc: Music (and choir); art; drama club	**Careers Education:** ASDAN: World of Work (ASDAN group)
Maths: ASDAN: Number Handling (ASDAN group)	**Humanities:** ASDAN: Wider World (ASDAN group)	**PSHE / Sex Education:** ASDAN: Health and Survival (PSHE lessons and ASDAN group)
ICT: ASDAN: Information Handling (ASDAN group) Inc: midday computer club	**Physical Education:** ASDAN: Sport and Leisure Inc: PE and games; keep-fit club	**Religious Education:** ASDAN: Beliefs and Values (form group)
Work-related Learning: ASDAN: World of Work (ASDAN group) Work experience at temple	**Citizenship:** ASDAN: The Community (form group) ASDAN: The Environment (form group)	**Modern Foreign Languages:**

FIGURE 8.1a   Page 1 of completed Key Stage 4 curriculum plan

Key Stage 4 Curriculum Plan	Name: Jasmir S.	Year 10/Year 11

Comments from Guidance Interview:
Jasmir is very caring and likes to help others. He has a great sense of humour. He is strong and fit and likes PE. He supports Manchester United. He is very interested in Sikhism and India. He wants to get better in reading and maths so he can get a job when he leaves school. He likes playing on his computer and wants to learn more.

Parents' views:
Mr and Mrs Singh are pleased with Jasmir's progress and want him to take accredited courses in Key Stage 4 so that he will have some qualifications. They would like him to go to a specialist college when he is 19. They are concerned that he might be vulnerable to bullying.

Individual Priorities:
Literacy: Jasmir has a small sight vocabulary. He finds writing very difficult but he has improved his typing using an Alphasmart.
Numeracy: Jasmir and his parents want him to be independent with money and be able to buy things from the shops by himself.
ICT: Jasmir loves his computer at home and he wants to learn how to use the internet and email.
Work-related Learning: Jasmir has no particular ambition at the moment but he wants to find out more about the Sikh temple.
Life skills: Jasmir's parents are keen for him to learn how to use buses.

Accredited courses: ASDAN: Bronze Challenge

Modules/units for the following year: ASDAN

Information Handling	Sport and Leisure
Health and survival	Expressive arts
The Community	Number Handling
World of Work	Wider World
Beliefs and Values	

Included in year/form group for: Music, Art, PSHE, Sex education, Citizenship, RE, PE and Games
Extracurricular groups: drama club, choir, midday computer club. Work experience: Sikh Temple

FIGURE 8.1b   Page 2 of completed Key Stage 4 curriculum plan

related learning may be delivered across the curriculum, should not require additional curriculum time, and should not be seen merely as a response to underachievement or disaffection, rather it is an essential component of Key Stage 4 for all students. National Curriculum subjects and work-related skills linked will give greater relevance to academic work, and more focus to career planning. Work-related learning in Key Stage 4 comprises three strands:

- learning through experience of work
- learning about work and working practices
- learning the skills for work. (QCA 2003)

The key skills for employability and enterprise are very important for students with learning difficulties who will face greater barriers than most when trying to find employment. Having a job is a vital part of financial and social independence as an adult, and should be the aspiration for all students. Some students may need to work in supported employment, but the necessary work skills will still be the same. Several accredited entry level courses include modules or units relating to the world of work. Direct work experience, enterprise activities, industry days, or taster sessions at a further education college, will underpin the work-related learning taking place in school and will help students with learning difficulties to generalise the skills into other contexts.

Never write off a student with learning difficulties just because he or she is likely to need supported employment. The student's ambitions can be moved to another level by developing basic skills and work-related learning. People with learning difficulties have many and varied personal gifts to bring to the world of work. Developing the skills needed for employment is in part preparing them for a satisfying and fulfilling adult life.

Recognising achievement at Key Stage 4

While the majority of students in Key Stage 4 will take GCSE courses there will always be a significant minority for whom these examination courses are neither appropriate, nor beneficial. Many of these pupils will have difficulties with literacy and numeracy, or have behavioural or social difficulties. To offer them more of the same in Key Stage 4 in subjects in which they may already have failed is to do them a great disservice, and wastes the talents which they could develop in other areas. For students over the age of 14 there are some excellent accredited programmes that can be used flexibly to meet individual needs. Most of these programmes include performance criteria that students must meet, usually through positive statements.

Entry Level courses

Entry Level is the first level of the National Qualifications Framework. It comes before Foundation Level, and is divided into three sublevels: E1, E2 and E3, with E3 being the highest. These sublevels are broadly comparable with National Curriculum Levels 1, 2 and 3. The aim of Entry Level courses is to encourage and recognise the achievement of a wider range of learners, and to enable those learners to gain recognised qualifications.

The Entry Level certificates are nationally recognised qualifications. Most certificates are made up of a number of units. Each unit is assessed separately so that students' small steps of achievement are recognised on the way to completing the full certificate (QCA 2003). There are no set rules about the selection or the number of units that should be included in a certificate.

Awarding bodies can create certificates that meet the diverse needs of learners at this level. The certificates can be made up of units from one or more of the entry sublevels, to match differing abilities across skill areas. Courses for entry level certificates do not have to be completed within a set time limit, but those courses that run in schools usually span Years 10 and 11.

The certificates are assessed through tests, assignments, or tasks. These are set by the awarding body which also assesses or moderates a percentage of the work. The remainder of the certificate is assessed by the school. Evidence of achievement can be collected in a variety of formats, such as witness statements, videos, audio, and photographs, in addition to handwritten or word processed material. This evidence often is put together into a portfolio of achievement.

Some awarding bodies offer pre-entry level courses that prepare students to take entry level units in the National Qualifications Framework. These courses are particularly relevant for those working on the P scales, below Level 1 of the National Curriculum. There are a number of awarding bodies that offer pre-entry and entry level certificates. Some of these bodies specialise in providing for entry level learners. All the schemes provide progression into higher level qualifications along which students can work at their own pace and ability level.

Figure 8.2 gives details and contact details for the major providers of entry level courses and programmes.

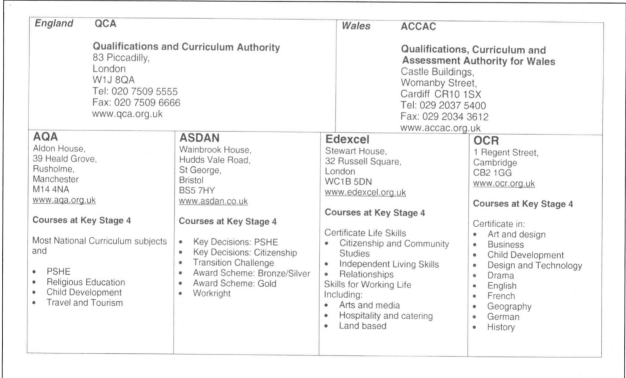

FIGURE 8.2 Accredited entry level courses and programmes

Progress files

Part of the freedom from the tyranny of the GCSE courses in Key Stage 4 is the ability to record progress in a format to suit the individual pupil. The Progress File, which has now replaced the National Record of Achievement, is the perfect way to celebrate and display students' achievements. In Year 10, students should begin to choose for themselves which work they want to keep as part of their own Progress File. Families enjoy seeing the File, and it gives them reassurance that the student is working hard and making progress. The Progress File can be linked in full or in part to the accredited courses undertaken by the student.

The Progress File is usually a folder, but one that will quickly become very full and very heavy. A more manageable format is the re-writable CD-ROM which can store a huge amount of information in various formats. Word processed work can be stored directly onto the CD-ROM, and hand-written work, drawings and pictures scanned in. Even music or speech can be stored as sound files. Practical work such as paintings, sculpture, or technology products, can be photographed on a digital camera and stored on the CD-ROM. At the end of Year 11 the work on the CD-ROM can be edited, and highlights put into a PowerPoint display to share with peers, teachers, parents and family. The CD-ROM format is a manageable alternative or addition to paper methods, and involves the pupil in developing ICT skills in the process.

Work experience

Students with learning difficulties will need a period of preparation before work experience placements are begun if the placement is to be successful. A video can be made of the workplace, with the people involved introducing themselves and giving a demonstration of what the learner will be expected to do. Students with learning difficulties sometimes are reluctant to wear unfamiliar clothes, so any special clothing or uniform should be given to the student well in advance of the first visit. Several preparatory supported visits will need to be made, each time lasting a little longer. Let the student wear the uniform for these preparatory visits, and he or she will gradually become accustomed to the new setting and ready for the full work experience.

One preliminary visit can be used to take photographs for a scrapbook with symbol supported text. The scrapbook can be given to the student to take home to share with parents and family, and will form an important part of the work experience preparation. Where students use signing to support communication, teach any new signs that will be needed in the workplace. Specialist signs for a range of work settings are available from Makaton, and also in the Signalong publication, An Introduction to the Workplace (Kennard 1995b).

Finding work experience placements for students with learning difficulties will require persistence and determination. Work experience coordinators will need to overcome ignorance and prejudice from people outside education. Many people may never have met a person with learning difficulties, and may consequently have some misconceptions. Initial problems often disappear once an employer gets to know a student as an individual. A useful starting point is to help the student create a portfolio of information to share with potential employers. The portfolio should contain a photograph of the student and a brief pen portrait listing his or her strengths, interests, and also those things that may be obstacles to participation. Examples of work, and short reports from teachers, will give the employer a fuller picture of what the student can offer to the world of work.

Support for students on work experience should involve a change in the nature of the relationship between the teaching assistant and the student. The pupil–teacher relationship existing in school is not appropriate in the context of the workplace. Wherever possible the student at work should operate independently so as to maximise opportunities for interaction with co-workers. For students who require a yet closer level of support, the teaching assistant should act as a colleague for the duration of the placement. Co-workers can take responsibility for training the student, and the teaching assistant can be trained alongside.

Safety is a major consideration for students with learning difficulties on work experience placements. One purpose of work experience should be to develop independence, and that would not be possible in potentially dangerous situations. On the other hand over-protection will limit the student's learning. A balance needs to be found between allowing students to take calculated risks and keeping them safe. For example, many students with learning difficulties enjoy cooking, and it is an important life skill. Any catering course necessitates the use of very sharp knives potentially lethal to students and those around them. Ideally the student should be taught how to use knives safely, but this may not be a reasonable option for some. Where there are alternatives to sharp knives that enable students to achieve the same or similar effect – peelers, graters, food processors – the same result can be achieved without an equal risk of injury.

Life skills programmes

All students need certain skills to enable them to function in today's busy and complicated world. These skills are gained from our parents, from other young people, and from school. Students with learning difficulties need these same skills, but they will take longer to learn and to develop a similar level of independence.

Greater emphasis can be given in Key Stage 4 to prepare students for an adult life as independent as possible. The life skills that some schools feel they need to offer should be tailored to meet the individual needs of the student. Schools need to look very carefully at the skills they teach, and whether these could be taught more effectively in other contexts. Any life skills programme needs to involve pupils working towards planned objectives as part of a group. Very few life skills are used in isolation, and a programme designed around just one student will be sterile and irrelevant. Most life skills can be taught through the usual subject and PSHE/Citizenship programme, and many Entry Level courses offer life skills modules that enable progress to be linked to nationally recognised accreditation.

Some skills are best learned in the home context, while others can be taught in school. Parents and teachers need to discuss carefully exactly which skills a student needs, and by whom those skills should be addressed. For example, if a student regularly visits a supermarket with his or her parents there may be little point duplicating this activity during school time. Moreover, the school can support the student's shopping skills by offering specific teaching on checking change and weighing goods.

Students often travel on public transport with their parents. Following discussion with parents, the school might use role play to teach the student how to ask for a ticket, and practise matching coins to fares in maths lessons. In this way, working with parents avoids duplication of effort and makes best use of a student's time in school.

There are aspects of life skills that the school most effectively can deliver through the curriculum. Basic cookery and hygiene are integral elements of food technology courses, and as part of a course it would be appropriate for pupils to shop for the food they need to use. Some local education authorities are developing supported courses for young people with learning difficulties on using public transport. Rather than providing transport to and from school by taxi or minibus, students are supported by trained adults to learn how to use buses. Such a programme gradually reduces the level of support as the student's independence and confidence increases. This kind of programme is ideal in supporting progression for life after school.

Personal care

In the past special schools taught pupils how to take a shower, and boys how to shave. The advent of the National Curriculum meant there was no longer time within the curriculum for such activities, and they were phased out. This is a good thing as these aspects of personal care are best taught as a natural part of family life. Where parents or carers are unable or unwilling to teach their child an appropriate hygiene routine, school will need to give the pupil some training in basic personal care, for the sake of both the individual pupil and the other members of the school community.

Some students with learning difficulties *and* additional physical difficulties may need support for personal care all through their time in the school. With modern sanitary products this should not be a barrier to full participation. As part of this support, students will need to be taught to take as much responsibility as possible for their own care, and gradually to work towards total independence. This applies to girls also, who may need additional support during menstruation. They may need to be helped, but that help can be in the form of verbal prompts, or the more physical support depending on the student's individual needs. The aim should be always to enable the student to do as much as possible for him or herself. Once dependent on adult support it is very difficult then to encourage the student to do things for themselves. Giving the minimum level of support for the shortest time possible is the best strategy to avoid dependence on adults.

Maintaining relationships with peers

Alongside the widening gap in ability can come a widening gap in social interests and life style. This gap may be because students are taking different courses but occurs also because of their changing relationships at this time with the pairing off of boyfriends and girlfriends. Students with learning difficulties may not yet be ready for this form of relationship, and may need support and guidance to help them understand relationships they see around the school. Distress may also be caused because the student with learning difficulties may be attracted to another student, but may not have the social skills or the confidence to make the necessary approaches.

The Circle of Friends will be a valuable support through this period of change, offering consistency and continuity. A new, smaller, Circle of Friends or buddy group may be more appropriate for Key Stage 4. The added maturity of students at this key stage should enable them to support the focus student both by direct intervention and by keeping a watching brief to ensure he or she is happy and safe in school.

Friendships also will assume a greater importance as students face new challenges. Regular tutorials with a mentor or form teacher will give the student with learning difficulties opportunities to ask questions, and to discuss concerns in a safe environment. Other teachers can help this process by keeping a watch on the student and those around him or her. If the student seems isolated, either in classes or in break times, staff will have to intervene. Self-esteem and confidence built up over many years very quickly ebbs away when a student feels lonely or rejected. Invite a group including the student with learning difficulties to help around the school by, for example, setting out equipment, returning books to the library, or painting scenery. Activities such as these will make the student feel included and useful. Working together in a group will also prompt interactions and conversations with other students.

Inclusion in extracurricular activities

Extracurricular activities are at the heart of many people's school memories. The school play, disco or concert that gave them their first experience of performing; the computer club that led to a career in IT; the rugby side that forged lifelong friendships; the outward bound course in the freezing Brecon Beacons: these are experiences that shape a life and build confidence and strength of character. Students with learning difficulties can easily miss out on these opportunities, often because of something as mundane as the organisation of transport at the end of a day. Advance planning with parents and with transport companies can overcome these obstacles, and enable the student to participate fully in clubs, sports and after-school events. Inclusion in extracurricular activities and visits is just as important an element of provision as inclusion in lessons. This is reflected in Part 4 of the Disability Discrimination Act where school sports, clubs, activities and trips are mentioned specifically as part of education and services (Disability Rights Commission 2002).

Sex and relationship education

Just as with all students in Key Stage 4, students with learning difficulties will need education and advice on sexual matters and on developing and maintaining relationships. Very close collaboration with parents will be needed as the issues around people with learning difficulties and sexuality are complex and often highly charged emotionally. Students with learning difficulties can be vulnerable, and parents are very aware of this and concerned to protect their child. The problem is that while the student may be functioning intellectually at the level of a child, physically they are fast approaching adulthood. Students with learning difficulties need information on sex and relationships just as much as, if not more than, other students.

Sex and relationship education sensitively handled can protect and prepare the student for the future. The information will need to be given at a level and in a form that the student can understand. There are specialist materials available to support sex and relationship education for young people with learning difficulties. Signalong produce an excellent pack on sexual awareness (Kennard 2001) that includes symbols, pictures and signs to support understanding. Initial one-to-one sessions are helpful in preparing the student for whole-group lessons. Specialist materials can be introduced at this preliminary meeting, and the student can respond and ask questions in a safe and private environment.

Summary

And beyond . . .

The two years of Key Stage 4 are about preparing students for making choices and decisions about their future. In these two years they change from children into young adults. Physical appearances change, as do relationships with peers. Young people who miss these changes because they transfer to a special school can never regain the experience. Adolescence should not be about being sheltered and isolated. It should be a time of calculated risk-taking, and learning about oneself and other young people.

The broad curriculum that is offered in Key Stage 4 keeps open the many pathways from which students will chose their future direction. We do not know what the future holds for any of our students and that is just as true for students with learning difficulties, who will be among the first young people with learning difficulties ever to stay in mainstream school to 16. This experience will bring new and higher expectations and ambitions. Post-16 education must meet these expectations, and the first step will be to listen to what students themselves say what it is they want. The challenge is not to limit their future by referring back to the way things were done in the past, but to let young people lead the way with their own ideas and aspirations.

9 The voice of the pupil with learning difficulties

The child has a right to express an opinion and to have that opinion taken into account, in any matter or procedure affecting the child.
(Article 12 of the United Nations Convention on the Rights of the Child (1989))

When the voices of children are heard on the green,
And laughing is heard on the hill.
(Nurse's Song, William Blake)

Parents, teachers, doctors, psychologists, therapists – adults always *speak for* the child with learning difficulties but rarely listen to what the child has to say. The United Nations Convention on the Rights of the Child (CSIE 1997) makes clear that we must begin to listen much more directly to the voice of the child, and the child's views must be given due weight when decisions are being made about his or her future.

Well-meaning adults believe they know what is best for children with disabilities. For too long the relationship between schools and children and young people with learning difficulties has been based on sympathy: schools must move away from the paternalistic, sympathetic approach, and begin to look at the world through the eyes of the pupil with learning difficulties. It may be problematic for schools to adapt to meet the needs of a pupil with learning difficulties, but those problems are as nothing compared to the problems faced every day by the pupil – problems of inaccessible lessons, chaotic corridors, dangerous playgrounds, insensitive people. The time has come for schools and associated professions to take a more empathetic stance, with the pupil with learning difficulties at the centre of thinking and planning.

Appreciating that each child is an individual, with distinctive gifts, talents, strengths, abilities and needs will help schools become more responsive to the learning needs of all pupils. Part of the appreciation should be an acceptance that pupils with learning difficulties have opinions about school, that they really do have something to say, and that it is worth taking the time to listen. Many schools are becoming more democratic and collaborative, with school councils giving pupils a genuine voice in the decision-making processes that affect them. By developing and opening up this process to pupils who experience barriers to participation, schools will gain an added understanding of pupils' perspectives, and the additional participation will increase pupil motivation and limit potential behaviour difficulties.

Developing the pupil's voice

Pupils with learning difficulties have to learn how to be active participants in decision making about their own lives and need support from the adults who work with them. A process of preparation can start before the pupil with learning difficulties transfers to the school. Schools give out a lot of information to parents and pupils, and they receive a wealth of information about a pupil's learning. Few schools ask pupils (especially those with learning difficulties) what they want from their time in the secondary school.

Secondary schools could ask new pupils:

- which clubs they would like to have available;
- the sports they enjoy playing;
- the food they like to eat for lunch;
- the books they are reading;
- the computer programs they find useful.

These questions could be in the form of a questionnaire (see Figure 9.1), made accessible to all through symbols or pictures, in addition to text. Such consulta-

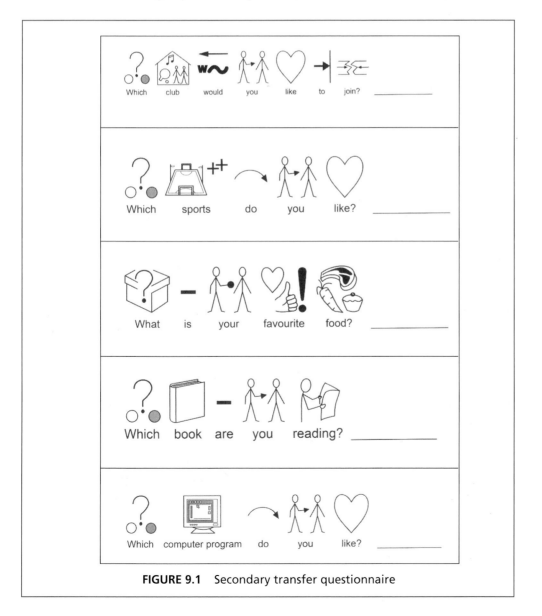

FIGURE 9.1 Secondary transfer questionnaire

tion at this basic level instils in all pupils an expectation of participation, and a belief that their opinions are valued. There needs to be determination from parents, teachers and other professionals to provide opportunities for pupils to make choices and set targets for themselves throughout their years in school.

Involve pupils with learning difficulties in group activities and discussions such as brainstorming, examining the pros and cons of a situation, and prioritising. This will support the development of pupils' abilities to make informed judgements based on thinking skills. Discussing issues raised in books with small groups of peers will help pupils develop understanding and empathy for another person's perspective.

Circle time

Circle time is valuable for pupils with learning difficulties in many ways. An emphasis on taking turns, affirmation, and particularly listening, supports the development of social and communication skills. If pupils have regular practice in speaking to a group and having what they say respected, they will be the more able to express their opinions and views in other situations, such as annual review meetings.

Reflection and self-assessment

Pupils with learning difficulties need to learn regularly to assess and reflect upon their own performance in school. Where pupils have clear and appropriate objectives for units of work, they can judge for themselves whether they have achieved the objectives, and say what they did and did not enjoy about the topic, and what they found difficult. A completed reflection or self-assessment record for each unit of work could be added to the pupil's Progress File. This information is then useful for future planning and differentiation. Over time, supported self-assessment will build up a pupil's confidence, and he or she will learn the skills required to offer opinions on his or her own work, and also on the curricular and social aspects of school. This reflection and self-assessment process will prepare pupils for setting their own academic and social targets.

A pro forma that can be used to support self-assessment can be found on the accompanying CD.

Advocacy

Many pupils with learning difficulties will be keen to attend meetings in person once they have been prepared in advance, so knowing what to expect. Pupils who are more vulnerable may find the situation too intimidating or distressing, and the use of an advocate is a way of ensuring the young person's voice is heard. The advocate must be someone with no professional or emotional link to the pupil. This person would need to spend time with the pupil getting to know the pupil's personality, his or her preferences and opinions about school and the decisions that have to be made. In the meeting the advocate speaks for the pupil, ensuring the child's voice carries sufficient weight. The pupil's parents must be consulted, and they must agree to advocacy before any action is taken.

The advocate could be another pupil in the school. Older pupils often are excellent advocates for pupils with learning difficulties, but they themselves will need preparation and training before taking on the role. The pupil advocate needs to have a very strong personality to put forward the views of a pupil with learning difficulties if his or her views differ from those of the professionals at a meeting. A shared advocacy between a pupil and an adult can also work well, with the pupil giving the 'cultural' balance of young people that the adult will have lost.

Parents as advocates

Parents are natural advocates for their own children but the wishes of the parents may not necessarily be in accord with the wishes of the child, particularly during adolescence. Their child's need for care, protection and support can override other concerns for parents. Adolescents themselves may have a quite different agenda, involving greater freedom and risk-taking. These differences must be addressed before important decisions are made about a pupil's future. Article 12 of the UN Convention on the Rights of the Child gives the right to express an opinion to the child, rather than to the parent. Whereas parents must always be part of any decision, the child has an at least equal right to be heard. Maintaining a balance between the wishes of parents and of the pupil may be tricky for schools and, again, preparation is the key to success. Potential difficulties will be kept to a minimum when throughout the schooling parents have been used to their child being consulted.

Annual review meetings

Annual reviews can be an ordeal for pupils, parents, and professionals alike. It takes time to help a pupil with learning difficulties to develop the ability to 'speak his or her mind' – without putting words into their mouths. It is not enough for them to be called into a meeting for five minutes, and be asked a few questions before being sent back to class. Pupils have to be prepared over a long period of time; firstly to become used to talking about how they feel and what they think about school; secondly to begin to believe that what they say actually matters to adults, and that action will be taken based on their views. A number of questions, such as below, prepared in advance of the meeting will enable the pupil to talk through them with an adult and have the answers jotted down.

- What do you like about school?
- What do you feel proud of?
- Who are your friends?
- What do you want to learn to do better?
- Are you worried about anything to do with school?
- Do you join any clubs or activities after school? Tell me about it.
- What do you look forward to doing in the next year?

The Pupil Comments form on the accompanying CD can be used to record a pupil's answers and can be presented to the meeting.

Some pupils will not feel able to attend the meeting in person, but their responses to the pre-prepared questions can be recorded on video or audio cassette, and shown at the meeting. Alternatively, a video link may be set up in a room nearby, through which the pupil can be asked questions. Even in situations where the pupil does not want to, or cannot, take part in the meeting, a photograph of the pupil might be given to each adult. This would help to focus attention on what is best for the child, and can help to prevent the meeting becoming bogged down in arguments.

A very straightforward 'What I want' form that includes a photograph again will focus the adults' discussion more directly on the pupil's priorities. A proforma of this form is included on the accompanying CD.

The voice of the pupil without verbal communication

Some pupils with learning difficulties do not have verbal communication, and so will be unable to contribute their views in conventional ways. No matter what their degree of learning difficulties, it is even more important for these pupils to participate in decisions affecting their lives. Sometimes it is assumed that it is not possible for pupils with no verbal communication to formulate opinions, and that participation is not feasible. In order to hear that 'inner voice' it will be necessary for the adults involved to know the pupil well as communication might be through signing, facial expression, gesture or behaviour.

It is not always straightforward to work out how much a pupil understands. Some pupils with learning difficulties have good expressive language, but poor comprehension. For example, pupils with Williams Syndrome speak well with a good vocabulary, but their understanding of spoken language is significantly delayed. Presumptions we make about a child's levels of understanding may not be accurate. They may understand much less than we think, and need much more preparation and visual support; or they may understand a great deal more, as with James in the following case study.

In order to hear the voice of pupils like James, with profound and multiple learning difficulties, teachers need to take time to observe how the pupil responds. Responses may include the direction of gaze, or turning the body

---

CASE STUDY	James

James lived in the north-west of England. In 1974 he was 12 years old and a pupil at a school for children who were 'severely subnormal' – as the school was then designated. James had cerebral palsy, and he had minimal voluntary control over his body. He had no verbal communication and limited facial expression. He spent seven hours a day, five days a week, either sitting in a red plastic wheelchair, or lying on a beanbag. He was in the school's special care class for secondary age pupils. Each morning he was bathed, and had a session with the physiotherapist. He spent the rest of the day watching a mobile, listening to music, or being fed.

In 1975 James was given a very basic electronic communication aid which he was taught to control by using a head pointer. This was the first skill that James had ever been taught. In fact James picked up the skills so quickly that he was soon communicating spontaneously and the adults around him realised that while he was disabled physically, his only intellectual impairment was his lack of education.

towards or away from a stimulus. The pupil might nod or shake the head as options are shown, or in response to questions with a yes/no answer. He or she may reach out and grasp objects and people, or push them away. Responses such as smiles, tears and laughter will give pointers as to how a pupil feels about different situations and people.

When the concepts involved are too intellectually challenging, pupils may genuinely be unable to express their opinions about their own future. Here they should be encouraged to make choices about day-to-day events: the kind of drink they would like; the music they want to listen to; who they want to spend time with, etc. This day-to-day decision making is vital if pupils are not to remain totally dependent on adults throughout life.

Practical strategies

The following are practical suggestions for eliciting the voice of the pupil with learning difficulties. There can be no guarantee that the strategies will work for a particular pupil. Try several approaches, or adapt them to fit the needs of your pupils.

Questionnaires

Questionnaires are a very useful way of gauging how a pupil feels about issues in school. A combination of words, symbols, pictures and photographs will support understanding, and responses may be gauged using simply drawn faces showing different emotions. (A symbol questionnaire is included on the accompanying CD.)

Smiley faces

Simple line drawings showing different facial expressions can be enormously useful in gauging a pupil's feelings about aspects of school. Happy and sad face cards or posters will give most pupils a way of telling how they feel just by pointing, touching or turning towards one of the faces.

happy

Computer programs such as Clicker 4 enable the faces to be displayed side by side on a computer screen. A mouse click or a touch monitor is used to select the face that matches how the pupil feels. The level of complexity can be increased by adding additional faces with different expressions, but the meaning of these additional faces will need to be taught before they are used.

sad

Signing

For some pupils with learning difficulties signing is the primary mode of expressive communication. Adults and/or other pupils who support the pupil with learning difficulties to give his or her views must be able to sign – and understand signs – at the same level as, or better than, the pupil. It may be necessary to involve a more expert signing communicator to be able to draw out a pupil's precise meaning. This is especially important for pupils with learning difficulties who are rarely very precise signers themselves. Their signs have to be read in conjunction with context, vocalisations, facial expression, and other gesture. An adult who knows the pupil, and regularly communicates by sign with him or her, is the ideal person to translate the child's wishes. Where no expert signer is available, a combination of signing and symbols, pictures or photographs is more likely to be successful than reliance on signing alone.

Symbols

Symbols have two distinct uses in supporting pupils to give their views. Firstly they can be used with or instead of text, to enable the pupil to understand information and questions. Secondly, they can be used to give the pupil a means of letting other people know what they want. This might be through touching or pointing to symbols, sequencing them into sentences, or putting preferences into priority order. Communication cards with a simple format can be tailored to match the ability of individual pupils and situations, from two choices to a grid containing over a hundred symbols that can be combined to give complex and precise responses instead of or in addition to speech. Symbol choice or preference sheets can be made very easily and pupils can colour in the different options, using one colour to show they like the option, and another if they dislike the option.

Traffic lights

All children are familiar with traffic lights and their meanings. A paper model of traffic lights is a fun way for a pupil to say how they feel about situations in simple terms. The pupil responds to questions by pointing to or touching the requisite colour – green if they are happy for a situation to continue, amber if they are unsure or just not too keen, and red if they definitely want the situation to stop. The colours can also be on removable cards that the pupil can lift up and put onto a representative object or picture. A traffic lights template is included on the accompanying CD.

Comic strip conversations

A comic strip conversation is a conversation between two people facilitated by the use of simple drawings. The approach was introduced by Carol Gray (Gray 1994b) for pupils with autism and related disorders, but it works equally well for pupils with learning difficulties. The drawings are used to illustrate objects, people, places and feelings. The pictures support pupils who in conversations have difficulty understanding the quick exchange of information. Drawing at the same time as speaking has the added advantage of slowing adults down, making them easier to understand. Both the adult and the pupil draw as they speak. No artistic skills are required, as stick figures are used for people and basic representations for everything else. Speech or thoughts can be recorded in bubbles coming

from the figures. Colours may be added to show different emotions (Gray 1994b). More challenging concepts can be explored through this additional visual component. A focus on the drawing also minimises eye contact during the conversations, which some pupils with learning difficulties can find threatening. In the example above, Christopher has drawn himself outside in what is for him a very scary situation – being confronted by barking dogs.

Draw and write

'Draw and write' is a technique where the pupil draws a person or an object, is then asked to talk about what they have drawn, and an adult writes the words around the picture. Pupils can be asked for example to draw things or people that make them happy or frightened in school. When the pupil is comfortable with the technique, the questions can be extended to encourage self-reflection, such as 'What do you do that makes teachers angry?'. As with comic strip conversations, 'draw and write' takes the focus away from the other person's face and adds a visual component to spoken interactions. By asking the pupil to draw first, the control of the ensuing discussion remains with the child and so increases the likelihood that his or her opinions are heard. This is preferable to merely responding to questions from the adult's agenda. 'Draw and write' also creates a paper document that can be shared in meetings. The following is an example of the 'draw and write' technique, by Christopher, Year 7, 'What do you do to make people happy?'.

Cue cards

Cue cards (see Figure 9.2) can be used to encourage children to talk more fully about school-related events that have happened in the recent past. The cards can contain words, for example, first I . . . , then I . . . , in the end I . . . , etc., or symbols, such as a stick figure for people, a tree to represent the world outside, or faces to represent feelings. The cards help pupils to structure their thinking and narrative with only minimal questioning by the adult. They can act as prompts for ideas about people, talk, settings, feelings, and consequences. Pupils, when practised in the use of the cue cards, are able to retell incidents or a series of events, and correctly include significant detail (Lewis 2002).

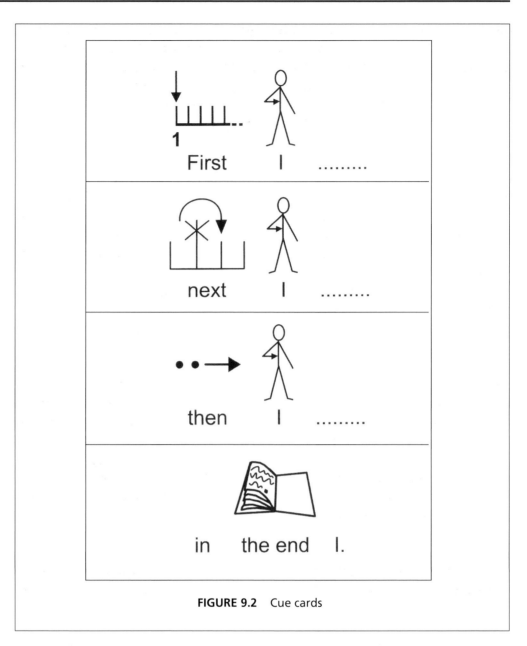

FIGURE 9.2 Cue cards

Mat techniques

Some pupils with learning difficulties need a larger format with which to make choices. Mat techniques involve a pupil moving their whole body to specific mats to show preferences. Mat techniques are also especially useful for pupils who have limited fine motor skills, but who can move by walking, crawling or shuffling.

Plain mats are placed on the floor (PE mats or carpet samples are ideal). Onto these mats are then stuck numbers, words, photographs, symbols or pictures showing different facial expressions. The pupil responds to a question by moving to the mat that represents his or her choice. If you are unsure whether the pupil meant to choose a particular mat, or whether they went to the wrong one by mistake, you could try the mats set further apart, sometimes even into the four corners of the room. In this way the choice is more definite, and the pupil can return to the centre of the room before making the next decision.

Speech and thought bubbles

Drawn coming from a photograph or a drawing of the pupil him or herself, speech and thought bubbles can be used to record responses. Sometimes seeing themselves from outside – as in a photograph or a drawing – helps a pupil to reflect on a situation more objectively. 'Me' bubbles (see Figures 9.3 and 9.4), with labels such as I can, I like, I am going to, I want, I don't like, etc., give a focus to questions. By focusing initially on positive feelings and then moving gradually to more negative statements, the overall response is balanced, and any negative feelings do not crowd out positive responses.

Masks

The use of masks can help a pupil to talk about feelings, literally from behind a mask. The mask may make a pupil feel more confident to talk about school and his or her priorities. Masks can be bought from educational suppliers but are much better if made with pupils who can then decide which emotion a mask should show. Plain masks can be bought, but paper plates are much cheaper and just as effective. Using the masks in role play enables the situations that pupils find difficult to be rehearsed, and different, more appropriate resolutions to be found. Pupils who do not like to wear masks, or who have limited speech, can be asked to choose a mask that shows how they feel about a particular situation.

Puppets

Increasingly, puppets are used all the way through primary schools to support development of literacy skills. Puppets are still likely to be effective with pupils with learning difficulties in Key Stage 3. Pupils frequently find it easier to talk to a puppet than to talk to an adult. This is because puppets have very limited facial expressions, while adults' faces change constantly and pupils struggle to understand the meanings behind the expressions. Even though they know that it is the adult that speaks and makes the puppet move, pupils still find it easier to interact with the puppet than with the adult.

Gauging strength of feeling

Where a teacher needs to gauge the depth of a pupil's feelings about a situation, a visual and/or tactile strategy will give a more accurate measure than words alone. There are several ways this can be done, such as:

- squeeze toothpaste from a tube with the amount squeezed showing stronger or weaker feelings;
- unroll a ball of string or ribbon;
- put dried beans into a pot – the more beans the stronger the feeling;
- hang smiley or sad faces, or tick and cross cards on a washing line to show how happy or how sad the pupil feels. (Lewis 2002)

A ladder laid down on the floor gives pupils a physical way of showing how strongly they feel about situations, and/or how much they care. Put large numbers from one to ten between each of the rungs of the ladder. The pupil is then asked a question and is asked to show, by moving along a number of rungs, how much they do or do not want something to happen, or how much they do or do not like something or someone.

Smart Alex (SEMERC)

Smart Alex is a computer program based on facial expression. On the screen appears the face of a child. The image can be configured to show a child who is a boy or a girl, with black or white skin. Under the face a grid shows words and/or

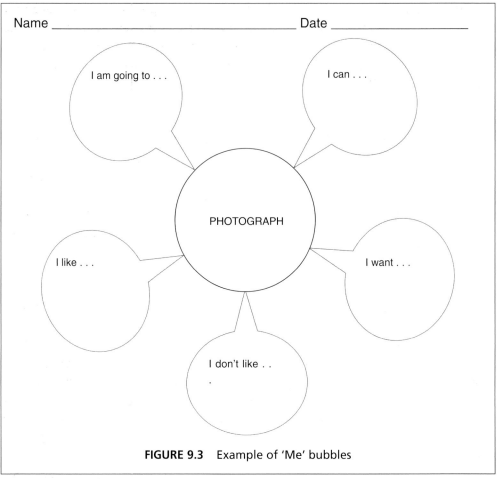

FIGURE 9.3 Example of 'Me' bubbles

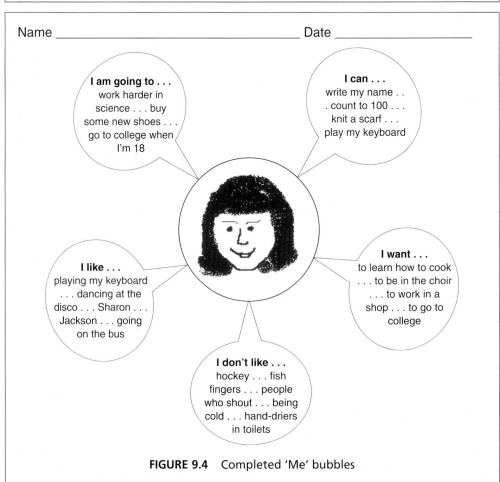

FIGURE 9.4 Completed 'Me' bubbles

symbols of different activities and foods. When a pupil clicks on a word or a symbol, Smart Alex's facial expression changes to show his/her feelings about the choice. This program is excellent when used as a shared activity. The adult can prompt the child by asking, for example, 'How does Alex feel now?', and 'What makes you feel like that?'

Concept maps

Concept maps can be used to help a pupil formulate their ideas by creating a visual plan. Words, pictures, photographs, symbols and different colours can be used to reflect accurately a child's feelings and wishes. Pupils with learning difficulties often have problems visualising abstract concepts, and concept maps make those ideas more concrete. Balancing the pros and cons of a decision is made easier in the form of a concept map, and is supported by the addition of colours, symbols and pictures.

Self books and films

An opportunity to be the star of one's own story can have a big influence on a pupil's self-esteem. Start with photographs of the pupil in different everyday situations. The pupil then can dictate a narrative based on the photographs. Other photographs might be included of people at home and at school so as to give a more rounded portrayal of the pupil's life. Other books may be created to support the pupil through times of change, and to help him or her make decisions. For example, a booklet on each of the different courses available for study in Key Stage 4 will give the pupil important information, and a choice made by handing over the requisite booklet.

By creating stories about imaginary children who experience similar problems to their own, pupils with learning difficulties can in a safe setting be helped to find solutions and explore alternative strategies. The fictional basis adds objectivity to familiar situations and events, and the story can be re-read as necessary. Reading about events in the third person helps some pupils to talk through the problems they experience in talking directly about themselves.

With digital video cameras now available in most schools a film of the pupil can be made in a similar way to the self books. If videos are to be taken of pupils, parents and carers must be informed and their permission sought.

Posters

A larger-scale format is more appropriate for some pupils. Create a poster with the pupil showing aspects of their life with key words or symbols and 'feelings' written in different colours to show how the pupil feels about each aspect. As with concept maps, the poster, by using arrows or coloured lines, makes it possible to link ideas and feelings visually. Thought and speech bubbles can be added to show the pupil's own words.

Poems

Poetry uniquely creates emotional and conceptual opportunities, for it frees pupils with learning difficulties from the constraints of sentence construction by utilising individual words and short phrases. Start by giving the pupil an object or a picture to hold. The pupil then dictates words and phrases relating to the object or picture, starting with descriptive words, and then moving to more emotional language. Acrostics are a good starting point as the initial sounds give phonic prompts, such as in the poem below by Josef, writing about his friends.

This poem says a great deal about how Josef feels about his friends in general, and David in particular. David has behavioural, social and emotional difficulties, and was not considered by Josef's teacher to be one of his friends but just one of several boys on Josef's lunch table. It turned out that while Josef liked swapping sandwiches, he often ended up with the other boys' rejects, and so lunchtime supervisors kept a closer eye on the table.

> **'Friends' by Josef**
> F – fun
> R – reading partner
> I – in school
> E – English bulldogs
> N – naughty sometimes
> D – David
> S – sandwich swap

Facial expression photographs and drawings

Facial expression photographs are available from several educational resource suppliers, but they are very expensive. A more cost-effective alternative is to make a set for the school using a digital camera. Either the pupil with learning difficulties is photographed making different facial expressions, and/or other pupils could be involved. This makes an excellent project for GCSE drama students, with results as good as anything that can be purchased. Laminating the photographs will protect them from damage so they may be used over and over again.

Drama, role play and dance

Drama and role play offer pupils with learning difficulties the opportunity to work through and rehearse situations and emotions with people they trust. Drama broadens a pupil's range of emotional expression, incorporates facial expression, movement, and words, and allows pupils to practise different ways of interacting with other people. In the same way, dance introduces pupils to an additional medium of communication by developing new body shapes, gestures and whole-body movements. Pupils with limited verbal communication may be able through drama or dance to communicate how they feel much more effectively and creatively.

Role play is a very powerful medium and can help pupils with learning difficulties to practise different and more appropriate responses to situations they find difficult. Some caution may need to be exercised, as a pupil may become distressed at reliving situations they find painful or uncomfortable.

Summary

Hearing and listening to the voice of the pupil with learning difficulties will take time and effort. When taking the trouble to hear what they have to say, by whatever means, that communication will always be worthwhile. People with learning difficulties know what they want from life, and those aspirations are much like those of everyone else – to be loved, to be safe, to have a home and a family, to be respected. If one of the strategies in this chapter does not work, try another, and another, and keep on trying. As with James in the case study, there is always much more to the pupil with learning difficulties than you could ever have expected.

References and suggested further reading

Alton, S., Beadman, J., Black, B., Lorenz, S. and McKinnon, C. (2003) *Education Support Pack for Schools*. London: Down's Syndrome Association.

Aronson, E. and Patnoe, S. (1997) *The Jigsaw Classroom: Building Cooperation in the Classroom*. New York: Addison, Wesley, Longman.

Booth, T., Ainscow, M., Black-Hawkins, K., Vaughan, M. and Shaw, L. (2000) *Index for Inclusion: Developing Learning and Participation in Schools*. Bristol: Centre for Studies in Inclusive Education (CSIE).

Buzan, T. (2003) *Mind Maps for Kids*. London: Thorsons.

Centre for Studies in Inclusive Education (CSIE) (1997) *Inclusive Education: A Framework for Change*. Bristol: CSIE.

Cheminais, R. (2002) *Inclusion and School Improvement: A Practical Guide*. London: David Fulton Publishers.

Department for Education and Employment (DfEE) (1999) *The National Curriculum*. London: DfEE.

Department for Education and Skills (2001) *Special Educational Needs: Code of Practice*. London: DfES Publications.

Department for Education and Skills (2002) *Key Stage 3 National Strategy: Accessing the National Curriculum for Mathematics*. London: DfES.

Disability Rights Commission (2002) *Code of Practice for Schools: Disability Discrimination Act 1995: Part 4*. London: The Stationery Office.

East, V. and Evans, L. (2003) *At a Glance: A Quick Guide to Children's Special Needs*. Birmingham: Questions Publishing.

Edwards, S. (2001) *Independence for All: Strategies for including pupils with special educational needs*. Tamworth: NASEN.

Fagg, S., Aherne, P., Skelton, S. and Thornber, A. (1990) *Entitlement for All in Practice*. London: David Fulton Publishers.

Faupel, A., Herrick, E. and Sharp, P. (1998) *Anger Management: A Practical Guide*. London: David Fulton Publishers.

Fox, G. (1993) *A Handbook for Special Needs Assistants: Working in Partnership with Teachers*. London: David Fulton Publishers.

Frost, L. and Bondy, A. (1998) 'The Picture Exchange Communication System', Seminars in *Speech and Language Therapy*, **19**, 373–89.

Giangreco, M. F. (2000) *Teaching Old Logs New Tricks: More absurdities and realities of education*. Minnetonka, MN: Peytral Publications.

Giangreco, M. F., Cloninger, C. J. and Iverson, V. S. (1998) *Choosing Outcomes and Accommodations for Children (COACH): A guide to educational planning for students with disabilities*. Baltimore: Paul H. Brookes Publishing.

Gray, C. (1994a) *The social story book*. Arlington, TX: Future Horizons.

Gray, C. (1994b) *Comic Strip Conversations*. Arlington, TX: Future Horizons.

Grove, N. and Walker, M. (1990) 'The Makaton Vocabulary: using manual signs and graphic signals to develop interpersonal communication', *Augmentative and Alternative Communication*, **6**, 15–28.

Jones, G. (2002) *Educational Provision for Children with Autism and Asperger Syndrome*. London: David Fulton Publishers.

Kennard, G. K. (1992) *Signalong Phase 1 (Basic Vocabulary)*. Rochester: The Signalong Group.

Kennard, G. K. (1995a) *Signalong Foundation Course Training Pack*. Rochester: The Signalong Group (restricted availability).

Kennard, G. K. (1995b) *Signalong at Work: An Introduction to the Workplace*. Rochester: The Signalong Group (restricted availability).

Kennard, G. K. (2001) *Signalong Sexual Awareness Pack*. Rochester: The Signalong Group.

Lewis, A. (2002) 'Accessing, through research interviews, the views of children with difficulties in learning', *Support for Learning, 17*(3), 110–16.

National Literacy Strategy (2002) *Strand Tracker for Non-fiction Objectives*. London: DfES.

Newton, C. and Wilson, D. (1999) *Circles of Friends*. Dunstable: Folens Publishers.

Office for Standards in Education (Ofsted) (2003) *Special Educational Needs in the Mainstream*. London: Ofsted.

Qualifications and Curriculum Authority (2000) *Schemes of Work for Key Stage 3*. London: QCA.

Qualifications and Curriculum Authority (2001a) *Planning, Teaching and Assessing the Curriculum for Pupils with Learning Difficulties*. London: QCA.

Qualifications and Curriculum Authority (2001b) *Supporting the Target Setting Process*. London: DfEE.

Qualifications and Curriculum Authority (2003) *Changes to the key stage 4 curriculum: Guidance for implementation from September 2004*. London: QCA.

Tod, J. (1999) 'IEPs: Inclusive educational practices?', *Support for Learning, 14*(4), 184–8.

Walker, M., Davis, V. and Berger, A. (2002) *The Tempest: A Play in Three Acts*. London: David Fulton Publishers.

Index